FIGHTING
THEM ON THE
BEACHES

FIGHTING THEM ON THE BEACHES

The D-Day Landings
6 June 1944

Nigel Cawthorne

This edition published in 2017 by Arcturus Publishing Limited
26/27 Bickels Yard, 151–153 Bermondsey Street,
London SE1 3HA

AD000188UK

Book design by Alex Ingr
Cover design by Beatriz Reis Custodio
Maps by Alex Ingr and Simon Towey

Printed in the UK

CONTENTS

INTRODUCTION

J OSEPH STALIN, the Soviet leader during World War II, said of the Allied landing in Normandy of 6 June 1944, 'The history of war does not know of an undertaking comparable to it for breadth of conception, grandeur of scale and mastery of execution.' Indeed, the D-Day landings in Normandy on 6 June 1944 were the biggest seaborne invasion in history. After years of training and meticulous planning, a vast army of British, American, Canadian, French and Polish troops – along with German Jews and other 'enemy aliens' who had fled from the Nazis – prepared to storm the heavily defended beaches of Normandy, and over a million men would be joined in one of Europe's largest set-piece battles in an area that is now full of tourist sights and holiday homes.

On the outcome hung the future of Europe, if not the world. For more than four years, the German Nazi dictator Adolf Hitler and his Italian sidekick, the Fascist Benito Mussolini, had held most of Continental Europe in their iron grip. Now Allied troops sought to lift that yoke.

It would be no easy task. The Germans knew the Allies were coming and built huge defences – known as the Atlantic wall – to protect 'Fortress Europe'. Many of the senior Allied officers planning the invasion had witnessed the terrible loss of life that had taken place in northern France during the First World War, which had ended only twenty-six years before. Although the Germans had been defeated by Anglo-American forces in North Africa and were being pushed back in Italy and eastern Europe, they were well-trained and well-equipped, and early in the war they had won considerable victories against what they considered to be weak and decadent democracies.

But, although slow to rouse, the democracies had considerable advantages when they went to war. Their leaders did not seek to coerce their troops into fighting, but rather to inspire them. John F. Kennedy said that British Prime Minister Winston Churchill 'mobilised the English language and sent it into battle'. For millions all over the world he articulated what the war was all about. On the other side of the Atlantic, American President Franklin Delano Roosevelt was also an inspiring figure. He had already brought his country through the Great Depression. Even though the American people had been reluctant to be drawn into the war in Europe, once it was inevitable the American people trusted Roosevelt to win it.

Both leaders made it clear that their war aims were not conquest. They expressed no desire to seize territory or enslave people. Even before the US joined the war, they had issued a joint declaration called the Atlantic Charter. It stated that neither nation sought any aggrandisement from the conflict. Neither wanted to make territorial changes without the free assent of the peoples involved. They asserted the right of every people to choose their own form of government, and they wanted sovereign rights and self-government restored to those who had been forcibly deprived of them. After the destruction of the Nazi tyranny, they would seek a peace under which all nations could live safely within their boundaries and seek to disarm potential aggressors. The Atlantic Charter even spoke of promoting equal access for all states to trade and to raw materials and worldwide collaboration to improve labour standards, economic progress and social security. The Charter was later incorporated into the Declaration of the United Nations.

The troops who landed on the D-Day beaches were familiar with the aggressive nature of Germany and Italy. They would have seen newsreels of the dictators coming to power, heard their belligerent oratory and seen their goose-stepping rallies. They would have seen Italy invading Abyssinia (now Ethiopia) and the Germans trying out their Blitzkrieg tactics in the Spanish Civil War. Germany had gone on to make repeated territorial demands before its armies swept across the Continent. In the days before television, newsreels showed shattered cities and terrified civilians and, nightly, American radio broadcasts vividly described the German bombing of London.

The Nazi maltreatment of the Jews was also well known, though the attempted extermination of the entire race was not known generally until the liberation of the death camps in 1945. But the young men who hit the beaches on 6 June 1944 knew very well what they were fighting against. Few doubted that Hitler and his Nazi regime were an unspeakable evil and many of them gave their lives to destroy it.

They would have been gratified to know that their sacrifice was honoured over fifty-five years later, though they would have been puzzled that we described the events of 6 June as D-Day. In military parlance, the starting date of any military operation is D-Day, just as the time it starts is always known as H-Hour. But that convenient designation has now come to stand for much more than just one more date on the military calendar. D-Day, 6 June 1944, now stands alone as one of the most crucial days in history.

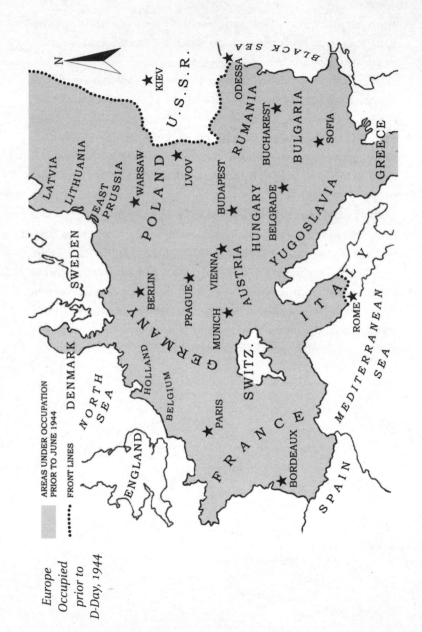

Europe
Occupied
prior to
D-Day, 1944

N

AREAS UNDER OCCUPATION
PRIOR TO JUNE 1944
FRONT LINES

BLACK SEA
KIEV
U.S.S.R.
ODESSA
RUMANIA
BUCHAREST
BULGARIA
SOFIA
GREECE
LATVIA
LITHUANIA
EAST PRUSSIA
WARSAW
POLAND
LVOV
BUDAPEST
HUNGARY
BELGRADE
YUGOSLAVIA
ITALY
ROME
SWEDEN
BERLIN
PRAGUE
VIENNA
AUSTRIA
MUNICH
SWITZ.
MEDITERRANEAN SEA
DENMARK
HOLLAND
GERMANY
BELGIUM
NORTH SEA
PARIS
FRANCE
ENGLAND
BORDEAUX
SPAIN

10

PART ONE
BUILDING UP TO INVASION

1

THE WAR AT LARGE

THE SECOND WORLD WAR had started in 1939, ostensibly over the German invasion of Poland. Its origins lay in Germany's humiliating defeat in the First World War in 1918. The Versailles Treaty concluding the war imposed crippling reparations on Germany. These led to an economic collapse, creating a political vacuum that allowed Adolf Hitler and his Nazi Party to seize power. Determined to make Germany strong again, Hitler began to re-arm and made a number of territorial demands which the democratic nations, ill-prepared for war, were forced to grant.

In Hitler's political manifesto *Mein Kampf*, he talked of Germany's need to expand to the east. In early 1939, Hitler decided to seize Poland, but there was a danger that this would prompt the Soviet Union – Communist Russia and its satellites – to come to the defence of its western neighbour. So in August 1939, Hitler concluded a German–Soviet Non-Aggression Pact with the Soviet leader Stalin. In a secret protocol, Germany and the Soviet Union agreed to divide Poland between them. On 1 September 1939, the German army rolled over the border into Poland, and Britain and France, who had military treaties with Poland, declared war.

There was little that the Allies could do for Poland, which was crushed in a month. The Germans then turned westwards. First Norway was seized. The German army then swept through Holland, Belgium and France in a matter of weeks. The British had sent an Expeditionary Force which found itself surrounded and it had to be evacuated from Dunkirk in early June. Fascist Italy, under Benito Mussolini, declared war on Britain and France on 10 June 1940. Paris fell on 14 June and an armistice between Germany and France was signed on 22 June, although sporadic guerrilla warfare was continued by the French Resistance, or *Maquis*, and Free French forces organised themselves in England under General Charles de Gaulle.

Britain was then in imminent danger of invasion. Hitler began to prepare Operation *Sealion*, his planned seaborne assault on southern England outlined in Führer Directive number 16 of 16 July 1940. Key to his plan was control of the air. Despite the undoubted bravery of the RAF pilots who fought the Battle of Britain over the skies of southern England, they were pitted against a much larger force. In August 1940, German bombers were pounding British airfields and radar installations with such ferocity that Britain was losing so many aircraft and pilots defeat seemed inevitable. But at the beginning of September 1940, Britain launched an audacious bombing raid on Berlin. This so infuriated Hitler – who had promised that such a thing would never happen – that he stopped bombing the airfields and began bombing British cities, an offensive known as the Blitz. Hitler's switch of target gave the RAF's Fighter Command time to recuperate. Soon they were shooting down German bombers quicker than German factories were producing them. This meant that the Germans could never win air superiority over Britain, the Battle of Britain was won and Hitler postponed Operation Sealion indefinitely. If Britain had fallen to Germany, no seaborne invasion of Continental Europe would have been possible. There would have been no D-Day

It has been said that, after the fall of France in June 1940, Britain stood alone. That is not true. Canada, Australia, New Zealand, South Africa, India and the rest of the British Empire were all at war with Germany and Italy. However, the food and *materiel* Britain needed to survive had to be brought by sea and the ships carrying these vital supplies were menaced by the German navy and sunk regularly by U-boats – German submarines – in what is known as the Battle of the Atlantic. Shipping losses reached their height at the end of 1942 and, in all, 2,232 ships were sunk.

During the rest of 1940 and the early months of 1941, the Axis powers – Germany and Italy – consolidated their position with sympathetic nations in central Europe and invaded Yugoslavia and Greece, where again sporadic resistance continued throughout the war. In September 1940 the Axis powers concluded a Tripartite Pact with Japan.

With Operation Sealion on hold, major land battles between Britain and the Axis were confined to North Africa, where Britain sought to defend Egypt and the Suez Canal – Britain's vital sea route to the east – from Axis forces that occupied the countries to the west. Battles there were inconclusive, though Britain did manage to take Italian East Africa – Ethopia – and return Emperor Haile Selassie to power.

The tide of war began to turn in Britain's favour on 22 June 1941 when, without warning, Germany attacked the Soviet Union. Britain suddenly had an ally whose huge manpower would eventually beat Hitler. On 23 June 1941, the Soviet ambassador in London asked the British Foreign Secretary whether it would be possible to open a 'second front' in northern France to divert Hitler's armies from the east. Although this was at the time impossible, the British responded by sending supplies to the Soviets, and in August 1941 Britain and the Soviet Union jointly invaded Iran, dividing it between them and denying it to the Germans.

On 7 December 1941, the Japanese attacked the United States Pacific Fleet at Pearl Harbor. The United States declared war on Japan and, in response, Germany declared war on the US. The American President Franklin Delano Roosevelt had seen the war coming. Although the American people desperately wanted to stay out, he realised that the US would inevitably be drawn into the conflict. From December 1940 America had been sending ships, munitions, food and clothing to Britain under 'Lend-Lease', a system whereby the US provided the materials of war, regardless of the recipient's ability to pay. America, he said, would be the 'arsenal of democracy'. From November 1940, President Roosevelt and Britain's Prime Minister Winston Churchill agreed that, should the United States be drawn into the war, the first objective of the Allies would be to defeat Germany. The Japanese fleet that had attacked Pearl Harbor was destroyed at the Battle of Midway in June 1942, effectively halting Japanese expansion in the Pacific. After this battle, the United States turned the whole weight of its armed forces against Hitler.

From the very first conference of the Anglo-American Allies held on 31 December 1941 in Washington DC, the US committed herself to a vast build-up of forces in Britain in preparation for landings on the European mainland. As soon as senior US officers arrived in Britain, their first job was to investigate the possibility of a cross-Channel invasion. The Americans feared a Russian collapse and began planning Operation *Round-up* to invade northern France as soon as forces were available. But the British dragged their feet. After two years of war, the British were wary of chancing all on one risky operation. Their worst fears were realised in a disastrous raid on Dieppe in August 1942. Some 5,000 Canadians, 1,000British and 50 US Rangers had been put ashore at the French port of Dieppe to test the newly developed LCT (landing craft, tank) and probe the coastal defences. Of 6,100 troops embarked only 2,500 returned, including one thousand who never landed. The rest were killed or captured. However, the raid had not dampened US enthusiasm.

Churchill himself was wary of seaborne assaults. As First Lord of the Admiralty during the First World War, he had backed the attack on Gallipoli in an attempt to seize Constantinople (Istanbul) and knock Turkey, who had sided with Germany, out of the war. The troops, largely Australians and New Zealanders, were caught on the beaches. Some 250,000 were lost before the remaining 83,000 could be evacuated. Churchill resigned from the government.

Nevertheless, in 1942, under intense American pressure, Churchill agreed to proceed with Operation Round-up no later than

April 1943; however, Britain's principal strategist, Chief of the Imperial General Staff Sir Alan Brooke, continued to argue that it was too risky. He proposed a more step-by-step approach. The Americans were eager for action and were persuaded to join in Operation *Torch*, the invasion of French North Africa. They made seaborne landings on beaches in Morocco and Algeria. The plan was to squeeze the German Afrika Korps, under Field Marshal Erwin Rommel, between US troops in the west and the British Eighth Army, who had already won a decisive victory at the Battle of El-Alamein, in the east. The landings took place in November 1942 and, by May 1943, North Africa was cleared of Axis forces.

Brooke also managed to get the US to sign up to Operation *Husky*, the invasion of the island of Sicily, and Operation *Pointblank*, the bomber offensive against Germany itself, whose aim was to weaken Germany's war capacity to a point where an invasion became a real possibility. However, there was deep discontent in Washington, where senior officials objected to what they considered 'sideshow' operations in the Mediterranean which the Americans believed were designed to serve Britain's diplomatic and imperial ends.

The Germans had foolishly squandered large numbers of men in trying to maintain a foothold in North Africa – more than 250,000 were taken prisoner. This left Sicily only lightly defended. At the Casablanca conference in January 1943, where the Allies met to discuss what to do next, Roosevelt agree to postpone opening a second front in France in favour of a more modest operation against Sicily and Italy, attacking what Churchill called the 'soft underbelly' of Europe. The Allies had overwhelming air superiority in the Mediterranean and in July 1943 they staged a seaborne invasion of Sicily with some 478,000 men. The British Eighth Army, under General Bernard Montgomery, and the US Seventh Army, under General George Patton, landed on two beaches, each forty miles long, some twenty miles apart. The Americans had already softened up the opposition by making contact with local Mafia bosses through the crime boss 'Lucky' Luciano, who was in jail in upstate New York. There were two German Panzer (armoured) units stationed on the island. Many of the Italian defenders were Sicilians who were unwilling to see their homeland turned into a battlefield for the sake of the Germans and put up little resistance. The success of the invasion posed an immediate threat to the mainland of Italy. Many Italians wanted to make peace and, as a result, Mussolini fell from power. Suddenly the Mediterranean theatre was no longer a sideshow. US military and political leaders threw themselves behind the Italian campaign. At an Anglo-American strategy conference in Quebec in August 1943, the Allies again agreed to the seaborne invasion of France, now codenamed Operation *Overlord*, but the British pressed for the timing of the operation to be left open. However, the Americans insisted that a provisional date of 1 May 1944 be set. They also pushed for a twenty-five per cent increase in planned assault force and a simultaneous invasion of Southern France, to be called Operation *Anvil*, even though the diversion of valuable resources would slow the Italian campaign.

On 3 September 1943, Montgomery's Eighth Army crossed the Strait of Messina and landed on the 'toe' of Italy. On 8 September, the Italian government capitulated and on 29 September it declared war on Germany. However, there was still a huge German force in Italy under Field Marshal Albert Kesselring. He counter-attacked when a huge Anglo-American force under US General Mark Clark landed at Salerno on Italy's 'shin' on 9 September. But after six days, the bridgehead was consolidated and on 1 October Allied Forces entered Naples. Other landings on the 'heel' of Italy sent German forces in the east into retreat too. But in mid-October, Kesselring established a defensive line, the Gustav Line, across Italy some sixty miles south of Rome where they halted the Allies' advance. In January 1944, the Allies landed 50,000 men north of the Gustav Line at Anzio. The landing met with little resistance, but instead of driving directly on Rome, the assault force stopped to consolidate its position, allowing Kesselring enough breathing space to organise a counter-offensive which, in February, nearly pushed the Allies back into the sea.

The main Allied force was held up by the German defenders at Monte Cassino, a mountain-top monastery pivotal in the Gustav line. The overall commander, Field Marshal Harold Alexander, decided to switch most of Eighth Army from the Adriatic side of the peninsula to the western flank. On the night of 11 May 1944, the Allies managed to breach the Gustav Line to the west of Monte Cassino, which was outflanked and fell to the Polish corps of Eighth Army on 18 May. On 26 May, the main Allied force joined up with the beachhead at Anzio and on 5 June 1944 the Allies drove into Rome.

Hitler had believed that a quick victory against the Soviet Union in 1941 would have convinced Britain and America that he was invincible. That victory eluded him. Gains were impressive at first, though. Attacking along a 1,800-mile front, three million Germans poured across the border, supported by Romania and Finnish troops. German armoured columns raced into the Soviet Union covering fifty miles a day. The Red Army was unprepared and partially demo-bilised. Within a month, half-a-million prisoners had been taken. But rainstorms in mid-July turned the roads to mud, slowing the advance. The Russians adopted the same 'scorched earth' policy they had used to defeat Napoleon when he invaded in 1812. They burnt crops, blew up bridges, destroyed trains and dismantled entire fac-tories and shipped them eastwards. The Germans had also underestimated Russian manpower. The Soviets had 150 divisions in the western part of the Soviet Union and German intelligence estimated that they could call up fifty more. By August the Soviets had actually assembled 210 new divisions. But many of these were wasted. The Germans captured another million men before they reached the outskirts of Moscow on 2 December and Stalin was preparing to flee. But the Germans were exhausted. They had suffered over 730,000 casualties, an unimaginable number compared with those incurred in their swift victories in the west. Hitler was so confident of a swift victory in the east as well he had not provided his men with winter uniforms. The lightly-dressed German troops began to suffer frostbite and the armoured column that had reached Rostov-on-the-Don – the gateway to the Caucasus – ran out of petrol, allowing the Russians to retake the city. And a counter-offensive by General Georgy Konstantinovich Zhukov forced the Germans to retreat from Moscow. German morale was low and the German troops were ill-equipped for winter fighting. Hitler sacked his generals and took over command. He ordered his troops to stand firm and stopped a rout. But this was costly. By the spring of 1942, the Germans had suffered 1,150,000 casualties on the Eastern Front. However, the Soviet casualties topped four million.

In the summer of 1942, Hitler began a new offensive in southern Russia in an attempt to seize the oilfields of the Caucasus. After retaking Rostov, Hitler split his troops, sending half into the Caucasus and half against Stalingrad (known today as Volgograd) on the Volga river. Starved of troops, the column heading for the oilfields faltered. The column attacking Stalingrad was halted and the titanic struggle for the city began. In September 1942 the Germans got within half a mile of the Volga river. In *Mein Kampf*, Hitler had said that the Volga was the limit of the territory he needed as a homeland for the German-speaking peoples. However, Stalin realised that if he lost the city that bore his name, that would be the end of him too. Both Hitler and Stalin poured enormous numbers of men into the Battle of Stalingrad, but the Germans never made it that final half-mile. The Red Army eventually surrounded the Germans attacking Stalingrad. On 16 January 1943, the German Sixth Army under the newly-promoted Field Marshal von Paulus surrendered with 94,000 men. Some 147,000 had died inside the city, 100,000 outside. Two Romanian, one Italian and one Hungarian army had also been destroyed.

Throughout 1943, offensives were balanced by counter-offensives in the east but, while the Germans were weakened by the stalemate, the Soviets honed their fighting skills. And in spring 1944, Zhukov began pushing the Germans out of Russia and the Ukraine.

But Europe was not the only theatre of war. When the Japanese had attacked Pearl Harbor, they simultaneously moved against Singapore and Hong Kong. They quickly seized southeast Asia, the Philippines, the Dutch East Indies – Sumatra, Java, Borneo and the Moluccas – and most of the western Pacific. However, in 1942, US and Australian troops retook Papua New Guinea and Guadalcanal. And throughout 1943 and 1944, US forces were continually involved in 'island hopping' – taking one island after another, usually against ferocious resistance, across the Pacific. However, this honed their skills in amphibious assaults and combined operations.

Although Japan had been fighting in China since 1937, the nationalist government under Chiang Kai-shek formally declared war on Japan, Germany and Italy on 9 December 1941 and the Americans sent aid in the form of the military advisor General Stilwell and 'Merrill's Marauders', US troops that had been trained in jungle warfare by the British. This was all the more important because the planes of the famous Doolittle Raid, under Commander James H. Doolittle, which bombed Tokyo and four other Japanese cities on 18 April 1942, four months after Pearl Harbor, landed on Chinese airfields. The invasion of Burma threatened India, which was still the jewel in the crown of the British Empire. It was noticed that the attacking Japanese forces usually got the better of British, Indian and Chindits (irregular British, Gurkha and Burmese guerrillas organised by General Charles Orde Wingate) by outflanking and surrounding them. So the British commander General William Slim adopted a new tactic. Instead of withdrawing, he left the surrounded men in position, supplying them by air. Then he would counter-attack, forcing the Japanese to fight with their backs to the encircled men. By May 1944, this tactic was paying dividends.

By the 6 June 1944 – D-Day – the Japanese were on the retreat across the Pacific and on the mainland of Asia, and their fleet was in port. The Italians had switched sides. Germany was on the retreat on the Eastern Front and in Italy. Meanwhile German cities were being pounded to rubble, by the US Army Air Force during the day and by RAF Bomber Command at night. The first 'thousand bomber' raid was sent against Cologne on 30 May 1942. Other German cities received the same treatment. 8,000lb bombs were developed. Cities were attacked with a mixture of high-explosive bombs and incendiaries, creating firestorms that burnt the heart out of them. Air Chief Marshal Sir Arthur 'Bomber' Harris made no apologies for the 'carpet' bombing of populated areas. He argued that the Germans had sown the wind when they attacked British cities: now they would reap the whirlwind. He believed massive bombing raids, on their own, could win the war. As it was, by forcing Germans to take a defensive stance, he claimed, with some justification, that he saved untold Allied lives when the invasion came.

2

THE ATLANTIC WALL

THE ATLANTIC WALL was the name given to the line of coastal fortifications built by the Germans that stretched from the northern tip of Norway to the Spanish border. The idea was to make any seaborne invasion of mainland Europe impossible.

It had its origins in Operation Sealion, Hitler's plan for a seaborne invasion of Britain. For an invasion to be successful, the Germans had to control the Channel approaches. So the German navy installed batteries of long-range guns in the Pas de Calais which were capable of bombarding the English coast in the area of the proposed landing sites. Hitler ordered the army to bring up its long-range guns too. The batteries were to be installed in thick concrete casemates to protect them from aerial bombardment. By the end of August 1940, the navy had thirty batteries in place, the army forty-two.

After defeat in the Battle of Britain, Sealion was shelved and the coastal defences forgotten about. Hitler was more concerned with the war in the east. He believed that if he could defeat the Russians, Britain would see sense and sue for peace. In the meantime, he put his U-boats on the high seas in an effort to starve Britain into submission. The U-boats sailed from submarine pens at the French ports of Lorient, Brest, St Nazaire and La Pallice, and the German island of Heligoland. These ports needed to be fortified to protect the U-boats. The Germans also refortified their North Sea ports, which had been stripped of their defences by the Treaty of Versailles at the end of the First World War. Fifteen naval batteries along the coast of Holland protected their approaches. The Channel Islands, the only bit of British territory held by the Germans during the

Second World War, were fortified in case Britain tried to retake them. And after an Anglo-French force had briefly reoccupied the port of Narvik in northern Norway in late May and early June 1940, plans for its fortification were drawn up.

However, the entry of the United States into the war changed everything. With America aiding Britain, invasion of the British Isles would be impossible and the whole of the western seaboard of continental Europe was open to attack. Suddenly Germany found that it had a static Western Front, which needed to be defended. It was only then that a plan for the comprehensive fortification of coastline was drawn up by the German High Command. Führer Directive number 40 instructed the German army, navy and air force to collaborate in the building of the Atlantic Wall. Soon after it was issued, the British commandos staged a daring raid on St Nazaire in March 1942, destroying the dry dock there. This was followed by the ill-fated attack on Dieppe in August. Even though it was a costly failure, the Dieppe raid alerted the Germans to the Allies' intentions. It was then that Hitler declared 'Fortress Europe' and the construction of the Atlantic Wall became a matter of urgency.

On 29 September 1942, Hitler called a conference to discuss defence in the west where he propounded his idea of a wall of concrete running from the Arctic Circle to the Pyrenees with 150,000 strong points and defended by 300,000 troops. It was to be completed by 1 March 1943. Although this timetable was thought to be hopelessly optimistic, Hitler knew a man who could do it: Fritz Todt, who had hurriedly designed the Siegfried Line, Germany's western defences, in 1936. He had also constructed more than 4,000 kilometres of autobahn between 1933 and 1938. Unfortunately he died in a mysterious plane crash in 1942, but the Organisation Todt, which bore his name, was still in existence. The plans were agreed on 14 December 1942 and work began on the designated strong points four days later.

But by March 1943, the Wall was nowhere near completion.

Setbacks in Russia and the intensive bombing of German industry had slowed its construction. Work was stepped up in April, but a report by Field Marshal Gerd von Rundstedt, Hitler's army commander in the west, said that nowhere were the defences up to the standards of those on the Channel Islands. He also pointed out that the speedy completion of the Wall was now a necessity as, with setbacks in Russia, Germany imminently faced war on two fronts. In Führer Directive number 51, issued in November 1943, Hitler accepted that an Allied invasion along the Atlantic coast was inevitable and the army, navy and air force were to make emergency preparations to meet it. Rommel was moved from Italy to France to take charge and, although he was subordinate to Von Rundstedt, was to report direct to Hitler. When he inspected the Wall, he found that, due to inter-service confusion, only thirty per cent of the required work had been completed. The problem was that the construction of the launch sites of V-2 flying bombs, a jet-propelled forerunner of the cruise missile, was taking priority. So Rommel began deploying an extensive system of field defences between existing strongpoints and, littered exposed beaches with belts of obstacles. He was all too well aware of the importance of the beach defences:

The war will be won or lost on the beaches,' [he said]. *'We'll have only one chance to stop the enemy and that's while he's in the water, struggling to get ashore. The first 24 hours of the invasion will be decisive... for the Allies, as well as Germany, it will be the longest day.*

As Allied deception operations led Hitler to believe that the invasion would come across the Straits of Dover – the shortest Channel crossing – defences along the Pas de Calais were strengthened. The Germans also believed that the Allies would have to seize a major port for any invasion to be successful. Fortifications around the ports were strengthened and demolition charges were placed in the harbour facilities so that they could be destroyed once an invasion fleet came into sight. By May 1944, the fortifications along the Pas de Calais, on the Channel Islands, around the Seine estuary, Lorient, Brest and Cherbourg were nearing full strength. This left a weak point along the Calvados coast of Normandy. This was where the Allies planned to attack.

Hitler's Atlantic Wall ultimately failed. But it did not do so just because of its weaknesses. It was fundamentally misconceived. Early in the war, Hitler showed that he had learnt the lesson of the First World War – that Germany could not win a war of attrition, especially one fought on two fronts. He had become the master of Europe with his *Blitzkrieg* strategy which employed fast moving armoured columns that outflanked and outran the enemy. These were supported by fighter-bombers which pummelled any strong point. Now he built a static line of defence, the very thing that had failed Germany in the First World War. Hitler had also forgotten another military lesson as old as war itself: that it is military suicide to try and defend a long static line. An attack in massive force at one point on the line will breach it and, once it is breached, the attackers can pour through the gap if there are no mobile reserves behind. They can then attack the defenders from behind.

In 1940, the Maginot Line, built in the 1930s to defend France's border with Germany, was simply outflanked by German forces who attacked through Belgium as they always had. It is better to have flexible formations that can manoeuvre in response to the moves of the enemy, pick their own battlegrounds and destroy the enemy there. But from 1941 Hitler had taken personal control of the war and would not give his commanders the autonomy they needed to manoeuvre on the battlefield in response to conditions. Not only that, he insisted that the Atlantic Wall be built as an industrial process with standardised components, instead of having each part of the defensive network tailored to its particular situation.

The whole plan for the Atlantic Wall looked back to the First World War. The concept of the 'hedgehog' pattern was developed on the battlefield of Flanders, where a network of mutually supporting strong points provided fire for their own defence and cover for the flanks and rear of adjacent units. The Siegfried Line, a German fortified defensive wall built in 1936 as a response to the Maginot Line, used the same principle, but it was not put to the test until late in 1944, when the retreating Germans used it to try and halt the onslaught of the Allies. But even since the Siegfried Line had been built there had been huge developments in weaponry and battle tactics, with the use of paratroops, gliders and amphibious assault craft. Despite these advances, there was no discussion about the need for a defensive line along the coast, which could have been defended much better by a highly mobile force. The idea of an Atlantic Wall, once raised, was simply accepted.

The planners soon realised that it was not possible to defend every section of the coast equally. So the idea of Strategic Coastal Defence Sectors were proposed. These were to defend areas where major enemy landings could be expected. Each was to be defended by one coastal artillery battalion with two or three batteries, naval batteries if they were available, one anti-tank brigade and enough Luftwaffe units to cover six to ten kilometres of the coast. Less vulnerable sections of the coast were designated Coastal Defence Sectors. Each was to be defended by one coastal artillery battalion with two or three batteries, one artillery regiment, one anti-tank battalion, one signals battalion and one engineer battalion to cover fifteen to twenty kilometres of coast. Behind them would be mobile reserves of armour, infantry, artillery and engineering detachments. In vulnerable areas, such as the Pas de Calais, these reserves were to cover eighty kilometres, while in Normandy they had to cover 350 kilometres.

Four types of coastal defences were built. The smallest was the Resistance Nest designed to defend against local attacks of armour and infantry. Manned by one or two squads, it was laid out around at least one anti-tank gun. These were flanked by mortars and machine-gun nests which were sited slightly forward, usually on the forward side of a sand dune to give a wide field of fire. Zigzagged communication trenches would run to the rear of the sand dunes and there would be air-raid shelters within the trench system. Rifle trenches would be dug along the crest of dunes to cover all approaches and dead ground, and the whole area would be surrounded by entanglements of barbed wire and fields of anti-personnel and anti-tank mines. Although many of these Resistance Nests were permanent installations on less vulnerable areas of the coast, they were also deployed as temporary defences where new fortifications were being built.

The strongpoint was the most common type of defence. These had a group of smaller positions in a diffuse grouping around a core of heavier weapons, such as artillery or anti-aircraft guns. Batteries would be mounted under concrete casemates. But where the emplacements were in the open, they would be surrounded by bunkers housing the command posts, supply depot and crew's quarters. The heavy weapons would be ringed by machine-guns, anti-tank guns and light anti-aircraft guns, spread out to make them less vulnerable to air attack, but still contained within a defensible perimeter. A strongpoint would be manned by at least a platoon, often backed by a local reserve. Ports such as Ostend and Dieppe would be defended by Strongpoint Groups. Larger groupings, defending the principle ports and river estuaries, were known as Defence Sectors. These had local reserves for immediate support and could call up the main mobile reserve. There were fifteen of these between Holland and the Spanish border.

Between each of these defences were Intermediate Positions which were manned by small detachments. They were not intended to be defensive positions, rather outposts used to maintain continuous surveillance of the coast. Then in the last months before the invasion Hitler added huge fortresses at the Defence Sectors where he thought the Allies were most likely to strike.

The German navy, the *Kriegsmarine*, concentrated its limited forces on the Pas de Calais, the main ports and off-shore islands, with the army manning the coastal defences in between. The idea was to produce a continuous, interlocking screen of fire. But it was difficult to co-ordinate this between the two services, so command of the army's coastal defences that pointed out to sea was given to the navy, while those inland remained under the control of the army. The demarcation line became the shore itself. Sea barrage fire in front of this line, whether provided by the army or the navy, was under the command of the navy; landing barrage fire behind the line was under the command of the army. Again this was difficult to co-ordinate, especially at night.

Navy and Luftwaffe (the German air force) radar stations were dotted down the coast to watch for an invasion fleet. However, the navy stations did not pass their information direct to the gunnery sites; rather it was passed through a central system, which slowed the artillery's response.

The first fortifications were built by the navy, while the field defences along the Atlantic coastline were installed by the army's construction battalion and garrisoned by its troops. But after December 1941, the construction of all the new main fortifications fell to the Organisation Todt (OT), which had previously built the German submarine pens. While the guns, armour and military equipment were supplied by the armed forces, OT was responsible for the procurement of plant and building materials, hiring subcontractors and the recruitment, deployment and welfare of labour, such that it was. The Atlantic Wall was largely built by slave labour whose welfare was of not much concern to anyone. Theoretically the responsibility of building the Atlantic Wall lay with one man, the Inspector of Land Defence West. However, army groups had special requirements,which were supposed to be cleared by Berlin.

This was a cumbersome process and, in the event, it was found it was better to have a local liaison officer who could advise the engineers. Distinctive features of the terrain had to be taken into consideration as they affected fields of fire and, in some places, mock landings were staged, to improve the effectiveness of the defences.

The design of the permanent fortifications was the responsibility of the branch of the armed forces that was going to man it. The army, navy and Luftwaffe had separate offices working on the plans. The result was that there were seven hundred different standard designs that were used in the construction of the Wall. Each had its own identification code with a prefix which designated whether a bunker, command post, combat post, observation post, signal post or support post belonging to the army, navy or Luftwaffe. Each was designed to the bare minimum specification. There were no frills. Even living quarters had no creature comforts. Thickness of walls, room heights, sizes of partition walls, corridors, door sizes, openings, room dimensions, everything was kept to a standard size. Where an installation had more than one standard function, various units were simply joined together. However, by 1944, shortages meant that wall thickness had to be reduced and gun emplacements had to double up as air-raid shelters.

All standard units were designed to be readily defensible. They had gun ports in the blank wall that faced the door, so that the entrance could be protected with direct fire. Each unit also had an emergency exit, a concealed tube or crawlway. This was blocked by a temporary brick wall that could be blown out with a light charge. Units were also fitted with air-tight doors, as the Germans believed that the Allies would use gas.

One problem with using standard units was the mounting of guns. On the Siegfried Line standard German guns had been used. But by 1944, the German armed forces had a whole range of guns. Many of them had been captured earlier in the war and were of foreign manufacture. Guns originated from as many as ten countries, and were of various ages and designs. This meant that their elevation and field of fire was often restricted by the standard embrasure, which had been designed for a German gun. The wide variety of guns also caused problems with the supply of ammunition. Twenty-eight different calibres between 7.5cm and 40.6cm were used. Vintage First World War 15.5cm field guns were common, though they were inaccurate and had a low rate of fire. However, after Hitler scaled back his naval building programme, modern battleship turret guns were used.

Fortifications were set into the ground – no roof of a closed unit was to be more than one metre above ground. However, this sometimes caused problems with groundwater seeping into the unit. Fortifications were covered with earth and grass to reduced their silhouette. Exposed surfaces were camouflaged with paint or texturing, and construction was hidden from aerial reconnaissance by camouflage netting. Botanists, zoologists and geologists were employed to produce lifelike camouflage. The construction machinery was covered with straw mats and plaited reeds, but it was practically impossible to hide the sites while construction was in progress.

Units such as observation towers were necessarily exposed above ground, so they were disguised as local buildings with false roofs and painted doors and windows. Those in isolated positions were designed from the outset to look like water towers or churches, complete with spires and buttresses. Some existing buildings were adapted and strengthened, and old fortifications were adapted to house modern weapons.

Hitler insisted that all fortifications were made out of reinforced concrete for propaganda reasons. It looked impregnable in newsreel footage. Its use also stemmed from his own experience of being in bunkers during bombardments during the First World War. Reinforced concrete was also found to be very practical.

Experiments were done to determine the thickness of concrete needed for wall and roofs, and corners were rounded to deflect shells and the force of explosions.

Where possible, fortifications were embedded in rock, otherwise massive concrete foundations were constructed. At first, high quality concrete was brought in from Germany but when Allied bombing began causing transportation problems ordinary Portland cement was used, along with local sand and aggregates. Although all fortification work was supposed to comply to the German standard DIN 1164 – and pamphlets explaining this were printed up in numerous languages – using local materials left construction wide open to sabotage. Forced labourers put too much sand into the mix, or even sugar, leaving the concrete much weaker than specification.

Doors were made from 40mm steel and embrasures were protected by armour plating that slid over the opening and locked in place. Rifle loops could also be closed. Added protection against rockets fired from low-flying aircraft was provided by chains hanging outside the embrasure, causing the projectile to detonate outside the casemate, and periscopes were used for observation.

The 'Lindemann' at Sangatte housed three 40.6cm naval turret guns which could traverse through 100 degrees on a roller path and elevate to an angle of 60 degrees. Ammunition was transferred to the gun room from the air-conditioned magazines through a flash-proof hatch to one of the two shell hoists in the gun turret. There were three storeys of accommodation and the emplacement was protected by walls and a roof three and a half metres thick. In all 35,000 cubic metres of concrete was used. In larger fortifications heating, air-conditioning and electric lighting were provided. The four main batteries in the Pas de Calais and on the Channel Island had accommodation for ninety-nine men, showers, a recreation room and a library.

Communication between units was by field telephone. Cables had to be buried at least two metres deep to protect them from damage and slack was left to stop them snapping when the ground flexed due to shock waves. Important installations also had radios in case telephone communication was cut.

Standard bunkers were also used to house field hospitals and dressing stations. There were water supply bunkers and storage bunkers. Others housed radar stations and the switching stations that relayed target information to the gun sites. However, German radar was inaccurate and liable to jamming, so the gunners usually relied on visual observation, supplied by spotters on their specially constructed observation towers. As well as coastal defences, the Atlantic Wall also comprised a number of offensive facilities – fortified submarine pens and docks for fast motor-patrol E-boats.

After the death of Fritz Todt, minister for armaments and war production Albert Speer had taken over the organisation. He was looking forward to completing some of Todt's more visionary projects – the extension of the autobahn system into France and the construction of a motorway from Norway to Sicily. But in May 1942, he was called into a preliminary meeting to discuss the possibility of constructing an Atlantic Wall. When he was asked whether it was possible he said that to build it, he would need some 400,000 cubic metres of concrete a month. This proved to be an underestimate. At the peak of construction, some 769,000 cubic metres was being used each month and some 13,134,500 cubic metres of concrete was used in all.

In 1943, fourteen Fortress Engineer Construction Battalions, four Engineer Construction Battalions, five Rock Drilling Companies and two Minelaying Companies were employed building the coastal defences in France alone. In Holland 20,000 civilians were recruited into the programme, along with 30,000 Spanish communists who had been expatriates since General Franco had come to power in Spain and had gone to work in France. These men were fed and paid, but most of the construction was done by forced labour sent from central Europe in vast numbers. At the height of the operation in May 1943, some 260,000 men were employed on the project in

France and Holland of whom only ten per cent were Germans, usu-ally working a supervisors. When those working on defences in Denmark and Holland are added, more than half a million men were employed on the construction of the Atlantic Wall. However, as the Allies stepped up their bombing of German cities more OT manpower was needed back in Germany to repair bomb damage and this soon meant that there was a labour shortage. Despite Hitler's insistence that the Wall be finished by March 1943, con-struction was still going in May 1944, following a new directive that all open gun emplacements be housed in casemates, although only twenty per cent of the concrete needed was reaching the con-struction sites. The work was not finished when, on 18 June, the commander of German forces in western Europe, Field Marshal Gerd von Rundstedt, issued a general order reassigning all OT work-ers from the coastal defences to salvage and repair work on the French railways.

By the time of the invasion, 12,247 of the planned 15,000 fortifi-cations had been completed, along with 943 along the Mediterranean coast. Half a million beach obstacles had been deployed, and six and a half million mines had been laid. Much of this was due to the energy and efficiency of Rommel. But he, like Hitler and Von Rundstedt, concentrated most of his effort on the Pas de Calais. In the crucial sector along the Calvados coast where the Allies landed, only half the planned fortifications had been built. Although many of the naval guns along the coast itself were in place, these were ranged far out to sea. Only a small section of second-line guns that could shell the beaches was in place.

Even so the Allies were facing a formidable foe. Von Rundstedt, who was nominally in charge of the defence of western Europe, had sixty divisions at his disposal, each with between 14,000 and 21,000 men. Although the Red Army was forcing a German retreat in the east, Hitler was convinced they could be halted before they entered Germany. The war, he now believed, would be won in the west. His whole strategy was to push any landing force back into the sea. Once the Allies gained a foothold on the Continent, the war was lost.

Between the middle of 1943 and May 1944, Hitler increased his forces in the west by ten major units. But the war had taken its toll. The divisional system had broken down and the basic operational unit was now the *Kampfgruppe*, or battle group, which was smaller than a division, but with no fixed structure. Infantry divisions had lost much of their artillery support. And although the armoured division were fully motorised, the rest of the German army depended on horse-drawn transport, with as many as five thousand horses to each division. Even the combat readiness of the armoured divisions was limited by the Allied bombing of their fuel supplies. Many German soldiers were reduced to commandeering bicycles for transport.

A number of Panzer divisions turned up in Belgium and France in the spring of 1944. After their encounters with the heavy Russian tanks in 1941, the Germans had begun building heavy tanks of their own. *Panther*, *Tiger* and *Königstiger* (King Tiger) tanks were introduced. These were impervious to Allied tank guns at over two hundred yards and could knock out an Allied tank at five times that distance. However, as the relentless advance of the Red Army continued these Panzers had to be sent east. Nevertheless, on 6 June the Germans had 16,000 tanks in western Europe, but they were largely grouped in the area between Holland and the Seine. South of the Seine they had only one Panzer division and two smaller units at Caen. There were six other divisions stationed in the area, but a number of them depended on *Ost* (eastern) battalions of prisoners of war from the eastern front who had 'volunteered' to fight for Germany. These were largely anti-Communist Russians, or Russians who said they were anti-Communist when they were starved and maltreated in prisoner-of-war camps. They had little motivation to fight the British and Americans.

Losses in the east meant that the army was having trouble

recruiting. Foreign workers were being shipped into Germany to release German manpower from the factories there. In November 1943, a programme was started to 'comb out' the remaining able-bodied Germans and put them in the army. Despite threats of the severest penalties for evasion, by April 1944, only 6,500 new men had been enlisted. More than half of the troops in SS divisions were under twenty, while 'static' divisions were manned with elderly soldiers and sick men. The situation was further complicated by the breakdown of the divisional system. No one knew whether a battle group had too many or too few men.

Luftflotte 3 (3rd Air Fleet) and IX Air Corps, the fighter and bomber units defending western Europe, had similar problems. Of the nine hundred planes on *Luftflotte 3*'s inventory, only 650 were operational, though there were a further 145 in Norway. IX Air Corps, which attempted to bomb the D-Day embarkation ports in southern England, had just one hundred planes. But shortage of aircraft was not the only problem. Despite Allied bombing, Speer managed to increase aircraft production considerably during 1944, but production then outstripped the supply of trained pilots. In May 1944, of the 2,155 planes lost by the Luftwaffe, 847 were downed in accidents not involving enemy action.

The Germany navy had returned its surface ships to their home ports and, due to the lack of Luftwaffe coverage, they did not dare venture out of port in daylight. In the west, they only had three destroyers, five motor torpedo boats, thirty-four gunboats, 163 minesweepers and thirty-four U-boats. And believing that the threat of invasion was receding, Admiral Karl Dönitz, head of the navy and later Hitler's successor, ordered the U-boats back into the Atlantic at the end of May. The navy also had a plan to lay 'lightning barrages' of mines at the first sight of an approaching invasion force, but the plan depended on the co-operation of the Luftwaffe, who refused to help.

Morale of the German forces in the west was not good either.

After many months – in some cases, years – of waiting they had grown soft. They enjoyed good French food and wine and entertained themselves with French women. They also had to suffer the corrosive effect of the disdain and sometimes outright disobedience of the occupied population. The growing activities of the Resistance disrupted everyday activities and made them wary. They did not feel entirely safe anywhere in the occupied countries. Orders were issued to give no quarter to Resistance fighters or enemy commando units, even if they surrendered without a fight. Soldiers who had been imbued with the idea of the nobility of their cause and the ethical superiority of the German race found it hard to reconcile themselves with the idea of shooting prisoners in cold blood. By and large, only Hitler's fanatical SS troops murdered prisoners with sang-froid.

On the Eastern Front, it was easier to motivate the troops by telling them they were involved in a crusade against Communism and the 'sub-human' Slavs. But in the west they had Slavs stationed alongside them, and could find no racial or ideological reasons for looking down on the British and Americans. One NCO was severely reprimanded for giving a cigarette to a downed British airman in full view of French civilians. Nevertheless, German troops were told that, in the event of an invasion, they were to fight to the death. Chief of the General Staff, General Alfred Jodl said, 'We will be victorious, because we must be victorious, for otherwise there would be no sense any more to world history.'

Jodl was tried and executed in Nuremberg in 1946 because there were men on the other side of the Channel who took a different view of history. In the end, the Atlantic Wall and the sacrifice of men who fought to the death on it was a waste. Jodl, who was close to Hitler, knew that there was only one hope for the Third Reich, the Reich that was supposed to last a thousand years. It lay, not in the Atlantic Wall, but in the secret weapons that were now under development.

3

THE WAR OF SECRETS

ALTHOUGH AT THE CASABLANCA conference in January 1943, President Roosevelt had agreed to postpone a full-scale seaborne invasion of France until 1944, the Combined Chiefs of Staff, comprising the US Joint Chiefs of Staff and the British Chiefs of Staff Committee, began planning the operation. Planners set about studying the disastrous assault on Dieppe and concluded that the strength of the enemy defences along the French coast required an immense concentration of power in the initial assault. Instead of dispersed assaults and commando raids along the whole length of the coastline, it would be better to make a single main assault. This would secure a beachhead, which would act as a disembarkation point, marshalling area and supply dump for the rest of the invasion force.

First the planners had to find a suitable place for such a beachhead. It would have to be within the range of fighter planes based in the United Kingdom, so that air superiority over the beachhead could be maintained. Airfields or sites suitable for their construction would have to be close at hand. The beaches should be sheltered from the winds. In the area there should be at least one major port and there should be good road connections so the invasion force could break out.

The Germans assumed that the Allies would land in the Pas de Calais, which gave the shortest sea crossing of just twenty-two miles. There were good beaches there and three large ports at Dunkirk, Calais and Boulogne. But the experience of Dieppe convinced the Allies that a port could not be captured on the initial landing. Between Boulogne and the mouth of the Somme there were half a dozen suitable beaches with good road connections inland. Although he expected diversionary attacks in Normandy and Brittany, Hitler was convinced that the main attack would come somewhere between Dunkirk and the Somme.

But the Allied planners found a series of suitable beaches in a sheltered bay on the northern coast of Normandy between the estuary of the Orne and the foot of the Cotentin Peninsula. There was no port there, but the planners found a solution. They would build harbours, code-named 'Mulberry', in prefabricated parts and tow them across the Channel. Once the beachhead was secured, Allied forces would be able to drive westwards, cutting off the Cotentin Peninsula. They could then take the port of Cherbourg and the ports of Brittany. Normandy was flat and suitable for airfield construction and there were good roads running eastwards towards Paris and the German border. The selection of a far from obvious site for the landings was the first big secret of D-Day.

The defeat of the Luftwaffe in the Battle of Britain allowed for detailed aerial reconnaissance of the area. Every inch of the coastline was photographed by dedicated reconnaissance flights, as well as by bombers flying over the area on a mission. Aerial photographs were used to build up a map with a scale of 1:25,000. Planes carried two cameras so that stereoscopic pictures could be used to build models showing the shape of the land, trees, hedges and German fortifications and strongpoints around the landing beaches and drop zones. These would later be used in briefing the assault force just before D-Day.

Aerial reconnaissance also revealed one of the Germans' secrets. Hitler's first 'vengeance' weapon, the V-1 jet-propelled flying bomb, showed up in photographs. A bombing campaign against the German research centre at Peenemünde on the Baltic and the launch ramps in the Pas de Calais, delayed construction and prevented them being used to disrupt the build-up of the invasion force. In 1943, aerial photographic interpreters spotted the beginnings of the construction of batteries of the so-called 'London Gun'. This was a gun with a barrel over 120 metres long which would blast twenty-five kilos of high explosives over 100 miles. There were to be two batteries of twenty-five guns, each of which would rain down ten shells a minute on central London. The United States 1st Airforce destroyed the site and the project was abandoned.

Initially, aerial reconnaissance had to be done at high altitudes, but in early 1944 the head of the Luftwaffe, *Reichsmarschall* Herman Göring, called his fighters back to Germany to defend it against the Allied bombing. This allowed low-level aerial reconnaissance from fast-moving Mosquitoes, giving far more detailed results.

But good though aerial reconnaissance was, the Allies needed to know about the construction of the defences and the strength and morale of enemy troops within reach of the beaches. A vast amount of information was needed about the beaches themselves and the landing sites that airborne troops would use. The defences there would have to be eliminated before the landings started and numerous objectives inland would have to be secured so that the beachhead could be defended. All this information would then be used to work out a detailed plan.

The French Resistance had already presented the Allies with a map and blueprint of the German defences around Cherbourg and Le Havre, the area where the landings were going to be made. This had been stolen from the German engineers who were building it by the French subcontractor called in to redecorate the OT's offices. Not only did the plans show the positions of gun emplacements, battery positions, pillboxes, machine-gun posts and trench systems, it also gave the technical specifications. Fields of fire, the ranges of guns, details of the communications and command systems, and the locations of supply and ammunition dumps were all shown. When it reached England, MI6 feared that it would be no use at all because once the Germans noticed that the plans were missing, they would change everything. However, that was not the way things worked under the Nazis. When the engineering unit that had drawn it up realised it was gone, they were so fearful of the consequences that they covered up its loss by quickly producing a duplicate. Aerial reconnaissance soon confirmed that the fortifications being built continued to follow the stolen plan.

The Allies got further information from the French Resistance. They would not risk going to see the defences themselves, which were constructed in 'prohibited areas', rather, they would travel around outlying areas, talking to locals who would see Hitler's Atlantic Wall being built while going about their normal business.

Many of the German gun crews were billeted with French families. They would be middle-aged men who, like their unwilling hosts, would have gone through the horrors of the First World War. This created a bond between them. Over a glass of calvados in the evening, the German gunners would moan about a pillbox that was a death trap, a commanding officer who was a drunkard, a unit that spoke only Russian or a vital piece of equipment that had not arrived from Germany. The Resistance would collect all these seemingly innocent items of information and send that back to an MI6 unit in London's Oxford Street known as the Martians. Piecing together the information garnered from these informants – some 50,000 of them – gave the Allies a detailed picture of what they would be facing when the invasion came. The information was so detailed that Allied units not only knew the intimate details of the officers and soldiers manning the targets they were to attack, they would also rehearse the assault for months before on replicas set up on training ground in England.

The man who had stolen the plans of the Atlantic Wall was named René Duchez, a painter and decorator who had taken a job in the Caen offices of the Organisation Todt. He had stolen the plans on impulse when the chance had presented itself, but normally he gathered information in a more systematic way. Posing as a simpleton, he would hang around in the cafés used by the Todt engineers and initiate arguments about building methods. He would volunteer advice, telling the engineers some old-fashioned way of doing something. The Germans assumed he was a collaborator and were happy to set him straight about the latest methods of construction. These were quite difficult to explain to someone as seemingly backward as René, so they would have to draw little diagrams for him which would find their way into his pockets. Every so often there would be an air-raid. The Todt men would run for the shelter leaving René and another agent, Henri Marigny, free to check out the defences. And at weekends René would take parties of boys and girls cycling along the coast. The Germans approved of such healthy exercise and knew nothing of the maps that René produced that were rolled up and concealed in the handlebars of his bike. Eventually he was betrayed, but when the Gestapo, the German political police, arrived at his house they found his wife, Madame Duchez, who appeared to be having a stand-up row with a man who was refusing to pay for her husband's shoddy workmanship. After a struggle, the Gestapo threw him out, not realising that it was René Duchez himself. Unfortunately, when they could not lay their hands on René, Madame Duchez was sent to Matthausen concentration camp.

Another agent disguised himself as a priest, as men of the cloth travel around at all hours of the day and night to attend to the needs of their parishioners. He was unmasked, not by the Germans, but by devout Catholics who suspected he had no right to hear confessions. Then there was a royalist sculptor named Charles Douin, whose work was to go around coastal towns and villages, restoring statues and monuments. Unfortunately, he blamed the English for the French Revolution and the execution of Louis XVI, and refused to work for the Allies. However, he was perfectly happy to spy for 'the King of France'. His work often meant that he would have to climb to the top of church steeples, which gave him a good view out over the flat countryside. As he went around the countryside, he would stop and, over a glass of wine, he would have long chats with the locals who often revealed details of construction work going on in the area, and with his artist's eye, he could spot fresh concrete, newly turned earth and the sun glinting on barbed wire. Fishermen were another source of intelligence. They saw the coastal defences from the seaward side and could sometimes be persuaded to carry a camera as they drifted by.

The Germans on occasion gave away information unwittingly. When they were going to test fire the Wall's guns, they would put up posters warning fishermen to stay away from a specific area. From the details, it was possible to work out the range and field of fire of the guns. Minefields were laid in secret, at night. However, when a farmer found that part of his land was off limits, he would go to the local tax office to demand a reduction in his land tax. All an agent had to do was sit there and listen.

The Germans also went to great lengths to conceal the designations of the units posted to the coastal defences. They removed badges, crests and identifying symbols. However, the unit's number was printed on the soldier's underwear which was given to local French women to be washed. When a unit was moved – usually, in the interests of security, at short notice – a forwarding address was given so that the laundry women could send the soldier's laundry on. When a German soldier died, he was buried in a local cemetery. The idea was that his body would be disinterred and taken back to the Fatherland when the war was over; consequently, his name, number and unit was marked on his grave.

Other information came from French men and women who worked as railway clerks, office cleaners, telephone switchboard operators. Vital snippets found their way back to London, where they were meticulously pieced together. Only as a concerted counter-intelligence operation went into action during March and April 1944 did the Germans begin to realise just how much the Allies knew. In fact, the Martians knew more about the Atlantic Wall than the Germans who had built it.

In January 1944, a unit of the French Resistance staged an unauthorised armed raid on a German command post with the aim of seizing documents. As only one of them could speak German, most of what they took was useless. But one vital document which found its way back to London, via Paris, was a copy of a report written by Field Marshal Rommel, who had inspected the Wall in November and December of 1943 when he had first been posted to oversee the German defences. He found it far from adequate. In some places the embrasures were so narrow they limited the gun's field of fire; in others, the emplacements were too small to allow for recoil. The Wall had been built by slave labour who had made many of these 'mistakes' deliberately. They had also skimped on the foundations, economised on reinforcements and weakened the concrete mix. This confirmed reports that the Martians already had, except they knew that the sabotage had been much more extensive than Rommel had discovered. Of course, the Todt engineers building the Wall knew the faults; to speak out, however, might have meant taking the blame, followed swiftly by a posting to the Russian Front.

With characteristic energy, Rommel set about strengthening the Wall. But as it would take a long time to fix the fortifications, he ordered extensive use of mines, booby traps and obstacles, turning northern France into what he called a 'devil's garden'. Again he concentrated most of his energies on the defences in the Pas de Calais. But in the weeks before D-Day, aerial reconnaissance revealed that he had turned his attentions to the beaches of the Normandy coast and the Allies began to fear that he had got wind of their plans.

Despite the huge amount of information the Allies had about the Atlantic Wall, they knew little about the beaches themselves. Would they, for example, bear the weight of a tank? At the time of the Dieppe raid, there had been a nationwide appeal for holiday snaps of French beaches. These gave vital information about the gradient of the beach, which could not be had from aerial photographs. French guidebooks were also trawled and it was discovered that that there were commercially workable deposits of peat on the beach in the Arromanches-Asnelles region, where one of the Mulberry Harbours was going to be put. Combined Operations Headquarters' scientific advisor Professor John Bernal was called in to do experiments on the load-bearing capacity of peat. After the liberation of Paris he visited an old friend, Professor Jean Wyart at the Sorbonne, who said that he hoped Bernal had received the information that he had sent at great risk about the tidal conditions and gradients of the beaches. Back in England again after the war, Bernal found that Wyart's information had been received, logged and filed away in a cabinet marked 'Top Secret'. It was never used.

Independently Bernal collected all the geological, biological and topographical information he could find on the Normandy beaches and tried to find English beaches that were similar. He discovered that the beach at Brancaster in Norfolk had nearly all the same characteristics as the landing beaches and preliminary training began there with Combined Operations Pilotage Parties in December 1943. COPPs were units specially trained to carry out reconnaissance on enemy beaches at night. They were dropped off the Normandy beaches by submarine, and rowed or swam ashore to take samples and make other measurements on the beaches. They also reconnoitred the mines and obstacles below the high-water mark. Samples were sawn off these so that replicas could be made which Allied engineers used in their training, so they would know exactly how to destroy them. This work was vital. Although these beaches obstacles would not prevent the initial assault force getting ashore, they limited the landing of the reinforcements, supplies and command structure needed to break out of the beachhead. Without them, the assault would stall and the landing troops would be driven back into the sea.

The Germans were, of course, on the lookout for commando

raiders, who were to be shot, on a direct order from the Führer. As a precaution, COPPs teams were also dropped along the Pas de Calais to continue the deception that that was where the invasion was going to come. Patrols by the German guards looking for commandos had another benefit: plainly the routes they took told Allied observers where the beaches were not mined. Even during daylight hours the beaches were reconnoitred from mini submarines which stayed submerged just offshore. Charts, harbour regulations, instructions for sailors and guide books were all used to build up a picture of beach conditions and new techniques were developed to work out wave velocities along the landing areas.

The beach at Brancaster was also used to discover what would happen if the aerial bombardment of Normandy fell short and cratered the foreshore. It was found that large bomb craters would hamper the landings. As a result only 100-lb bombs, with instantaneous fuses so they did not go off once the troops were ashore, were used during the landings.

The problem was that the Germans knew that the Allies were coming. Even though it seemed self-evident that they would attack sooner or later, the Western Allies encouraged the notion. In Operation *Cockade*, British intelligence actively fed information to the Germans that the Allies intend to attack somewhere along the Atlantic coast. The idea was to force the Germans to tie up German men and munitions in western Europe, relieving pressure on the Red Army in the east and the Allied forces fighting their way up the Italian peninsula from the south.

The central ploy for the Allied intelligence was to keep the Germans thinking that the landings were going to come at the Pas de Calais, so that they would concentrate their forces there. This would be difficult as the Germans already knew that the British were masters of deception. During the First World War, Field Marshal Edmund Allenby's intelligence officer Colonel Richard Meinertzhagen had dropped a bloodstained haversack, seemingly by accident, in front of a Turkish patrol in Palestine in 1917. Frantic radio messages intercepted and deciphered talked of Meinertzhagen being court-martialled for negligence. This convinced the Turks that the bogus plans in the haversack were true, leading to Allenby's decisive victory over the Turks in the Battle of Gaza.

More recently, the body of the fictitious 'Major William Martin' of the Royal Marines – 'The Man Who Never Was' – was dumped in the Atlantic to wash ashore in the Gulf of Cadiz. The Germans overheard British radio messages concerning the missing Major and his briefcase which was said to contain highly classified material. They persuaded the Chief of the Staff of the Spanish navy, who was sympathetic to Hitler, to let them examine the documents, before resealing them and handing them back to the British. This led them to expect an invasion in Sardinia, with a diversionary attack in Greece, rather than the landings that came in Sicily.

Consequently, intelligence officers were asked to keep a close watch on the Pas de Calais to make sure that the Germans were still building up their strength there. The Allies also needed to know that there was a minimal amount of activity in Normandy. If the Germans were ready and waiting, as they had been at Dieppe, Operation Overlord had the potential of turning into the biggest military disaster the world had ever seen.

When it came to deception, the Allies still had a couple of tricks up their sleeves. First there was Ultra. This was the code-breaking system developed by Bletchley Park that deciphered top-level German military communications encrypted in the Enigma code, which the Germans still thought was unbreakable. Bletchley Park were able to tell the intelligence officers spreading disinformation whether their deception was working on the enemy.

Aiding the Allies was the rivalry between the *Abwehr*, German military intelligence, and the *Sicherheitsdienst*, or SD, the intelligence wing of the SS and the Nazi Party. Head of the SD, and one of the authors of the 'Final Solution', Reinhard Heydrich aimed to take over the Abwehr and get rid of its chief Admiral Wilhelm Canaris, a known anti-Nazi. But Heydrich was assassinated in Prague in 1942. SS chief Heinrich Himmler also sought to get rid of Canaris, but Canaris had secret information on Himmler so the SS could not move against him directly. Canaris was only discredited after a high-ranking defection from the Abwehr in January 1944. The Abwehr was then taken over by the SD. Canaris was executed on 9 April 1945, as one of the *Schwarze Kapelle* conspirators who had tried to assassinate Hitler in the *Wolfsschanze*, the Wolf's Lair, his East Prussian headquarters, in July 1944. However, the new head of the SD's military intelligence wing, as the Abwehr had become, was, unbeknownst to the authorities, another member of the Schwarze Kapelle and a loyal follower of Canaris.

In an attempt to increase their influence over Hitler, the rival groups within German intelligence inflated their estimates of the enemy's strength, leading the Führer to believe that the Allies had between eighty-five and ninety divisions available for the invasion. In fact, they had just thirty-five. This played into the hands of Allied counter-intelligence who flooded the airwaves with messages concerning the non-existent First United States Army Group (FUSAG) and the equally mythical British Fourth Army.

Radio intercepts about these fictitious armies were backed with reports from Germany spies in Britain. This was easy to organise as Nazi attempts at espionage in Britain were extraordinarily inept. The Germans sent agents to Britain who could not speak English fluently and knew nothing about the country. They were supposed to mingle with the large population of foreigners who had fled Nazi persecution. But the areas where the invasion force was being mustered were closed to foreigners and they were easily picked up. Most never got that far. They were arrested on the beaches. Many were eager to give themselves up.

In March 1944, a German agent claiming to be a leading figure in the Belgian Resistance turned up at the British Embassy in neutral Sweden. He was on the run, he said, and the Germans had put a price on his head. To prove his story, he produced newspaper cuttings from the German-controlled Belgian press showing his photograph. This immediately alerted the British. What genuine resistance fighter on the run would carry incriminating newspaper cuttings with him as he fled across occupied Europe? He was flown to Scotland, where he was released to see if he would lead MI5 to other contacts. When it was clear that he was working on his own, he was arrested. Notes on shipping movements and bomb damage were found on him. These were enough to earn him a death sentence at his trial at the Old Bailey on 26 May 1944.

Before the Second World War, the Germans had installed two spy networks in the UK. One was a network of domestic servants. They were to report back anything of importance they heard or saw, but their main role was as a screen to distract the attention of MI5 and Scotland Yard's Special Branch from the professional agents of the Abwehr. Before they were despatched to Britain, the Abwehr sent their agents to a special school in Hamburg, where they were trained to look and behave like Englishmen. Their instructor, an Oxford graduate, told them that their best cover was to create an aura of respectability, and respectability in Britain depended on having a healthy bank balance. He taught his spies to open a Post Office savings account when they arrived in Britain and deposit all the Abwehr funds they had brought with them in it. They should go to the police and report the loss of the account book, mentioning how much was in it. This, he said, would be enough to convince the police that they were respectable citizens. However, the instructor was an MI6 plant and, the day war broke out, the British police had a list of practically every Abwehr agent in the country.

Key to the British counter-intelligence operation was a Canadian called Snow. He was an electrical engineer, but he fancied himself as a spy. First he offered his services to British Naval Intelligence in

1936, then he approached MI6. Both turned him down. So he offered his services to the Abwehr. Naturally MI5 had been keeping an eye on him and, the day after war was declared, he was picked up. It was suggested to him that he might like to become a double agent. As the only other alternative was a short drop at the end of a long rope, he agreed. Snow was in radio contact with the Abwehr and his handlers in Hamburg regularly informed him of agents they were sending. He passed this information on to the British authorities and they, too, were picked up.

The Germans had more success in occupied France where they could pick up British agents and members of the French Resistance. As D-Day approached, the Allies had to tell the Maquis of their plans so that they could co-ordinate the assault with the sabotage activities of the Resistance and minimise civilian casualties. German intelligence in France discovered the date of the invasion this way. But the prime task of German intelligence operations in France was to track down and kill the Resistance, not to interrogate them, and the information they discovered was lost in the fog of Allied deception.

Even though by 1944 the Red Army was moving in relentlessly from the east and the Allies were moving inexorably up the Italian peninsular, Hitler was still convinced he could win the war. With his V-1s and his London Guns, he could pummel Britain into surrender. Although the Allied bombing campaign was taking its toll, especially on the Luftwaffe, war production had increase tenfold since 1940 and there was no crisis of supply. He had tanks and guns that were superior to anything the Allies possessed, and an army of ten million battle-hardened troops. Jet fighters were coming into service that could outfly any Allied plane and the V-2 – the first modern ballistic missile – was in production. To prevent London being turned into a heap of smoking rubble, the Allies would have to take out the launching sites in the Pas de Calais. This was another reason Hitler was convinced that the Allied assault would come there and why it was protected by the strongest sector of the Atlantic Wall. Behind it, he kept his most powerful defensive force, the awesome Fifteenth Army.

It was very much in the interest of the Allies to let Hitler go on believing this and a massive deception operation was set in action. The overall plan to deceive the Germans in the Second World War was Operation *Jael*, after the Old Testament story of the wife of Heber the Kenite who persuaded the commander-in-chief of the Canaanite army that he was safe in her tent then, when he was asleep, drove a tent-peg through his head. The deception plan surrounding D-Day was called *Bodyguard* after a remark by Churchill at the Tehran Conference between Churchill, Roosevelt and Stalin in November 1943, where Stalin agreed to an eastern offensive to coincide with the Normandy landings. Churchill said, 'In war time, truth is so precious that she should always be attended by a bodyguard of lies.' Bodyguard itself consisted of two parts, *Zeppelin* and *Fortitude*. Zeppelin was the operation to convince the Germans that the threat lay to the south or south-east. There was a real danger to the Reich in this area. Since the failure of the German invasion of Russia, Hungary had tried to change sides and both Bulgaria and Romania were trying to pull out of their treaties with the Axis powers. Zeppelin tried to convince Hitler that there would be an Anglo-Soviet attack on Romania from the Black Sea, an Anglo-American assault on Trieste and a British attack through Greece. From there, the Allies would move on through central Europe and Austria into southern Germany. Key to Zeppelin was the so-called 'Cicero Affair'. A Turk named Elyesa Bazna told the Germans that he had obtained the keys to the despatch boxes in the British Embassy in Germany. He photographed the contents and passed over copies of highly classified secret documents. At first, there was some doubt in the minds of Germany intelligence about whether 'Cicero' was a plant, but the Germans became convinced when the British began to make a fuss about security at the embassy. Bazna was all the more convincing as it appears he was a genuine spy, but his activities were known to British intelligence and, unbeknownst to him, the despatch boxes were seeded with misinformation. As a result, Hitler reinforced the Balkans with twenty-five divisions that could have been in France on D-Day.

The other leg of the campaign of deception, Operation Fortitude, had three parts. Fortitude North tried to convince the Germans that the invasion was coming in Norway. Sweden, until then neutral, would come into the war on the Allied side. This would allow the Allies to land in Denmark and from there attack northern Germany. Fortitude South sought to confirm the idea in Hitler's mind that the attack would come in the Pas de Calais or the coast of Belgium. Then there was Fortitude South II, also known as Rosebud, which continued after D-Day. This was largely a radio operation designed to convince the Germans that the D-Day landings were merely a feint and that the real invasion of the Pas de Calais was still to come.

Bodyguard was directed at Hitler personally. As the war progressed, he took more control away from his generals and exercised absolute authority from his fortified headquarters at Berchtesgaden in Bavaria and, chiefly, the Wolf's Lair at Rastenburg in East Prussia. He never went to the front or visited bombed cities, preferring to run his campaigns from maps and seeing no one but a handful of staff officers. So if a campaign of deception convinced Hitler that was all that mattered.

The thrust of the campaign was to make Hitler believe that, if the Allies were going to invade France, they could not do so before July 1944, but that the attack was more likely to occur in the Balkans or Norway. The idea was to get him to disperse his forces around the perimeter of his empire. And Hitler fell for it. As Von Rundstedt said, the 'Bohemian corporal', as he contemptuously called Hitler, would try to hold on to everything and so, in the end, would lose everything.

The Allies played on Hitler's growing paranoia. He was to be led to believe that he was hemmed in on all sides by his enemy and he would never know where or when they would attack. He was also led to believe that when the invasion of France came, the main force would strike across the Straits of Dover at the Pas de Calais, though there would be diversionary attacks elsewhere – in the Calvados region of Normandy, for example. It was vital that, even after the Allies had committed everything to the beaches at Normandy, Hitler keep his Fifteenth Army in the Pas de Calais, waiting for an invasion there that would never come. Using Ultra, at any time the Allies could see just how well their deception plans were working.

Although Hitler relied solely on his own intuition, Von Rundstedt's more objective analysis of the situation also led him to conclude that the Allies would strike at the Pas de Calais. As the Straits of Dover offered the shortest cross-Channel route, there could be a quicker turnaround of landing craft and, thus, a quicker build-up of the beachhead. The Allies could give an assault force there maximum air cover. Planes would be spared a long flight from their airfields in England, meaning they could spend longer over the battlefield. The Pas de Calais also offered the shortest route to the main objective – Germany itself. Von Rundstedt reckoned that, if the Allies made a successful landing in the Pas de Calais, it would take them just five days to reach the Rhine with catastrophic effect on the morale of the Wehrmacht and the German people. On the way, the Allies could destroy the sites of the new weapons that were threatening London and there was every chance that they would seize at least one major port intact.

Knowing that the possession of a port would be vital to any invasion, Von Rundstedt ruled out the possibility of an attack on Normandy. The two harbours there, Cherbourg and Le Havre, were bristling with demolition charges. If an invasion fleet attempted the hundred-mile crossing from the English coast, it was bound to be spotted by radar, reconnaissance aircraft or German high-speed

E-boat patrols. By the time the invasion fleet reached the Normandy coast, demolition charges would be fired and the ports put out of action. However, if the Allies made a dash across the Straits of Dover, they might be able to capture Calais, Dunkirk or Boulogne before the Germans had time to blow the port facilities up.

Admiral Theodor Krancke, commander of the German navy Group West, also believed that the Allies would have to land near a large port. After studying Allied amphibious landings, he believed that beach obstacles and coastal defences could hold them off. Any attack would have to come at night at high tide, he thought, so that the landing craft could sail over the obstacles. An attack would have to be mounted away from cliffs and reefs where there might be awkward cross-currents, in conditions were the swell was less that two metres, with wind speeds of no more than thirty miles an hour and visibility of at least 4,500 metres.

Rommel disagreed. To overcome the beach obstacles, he believed that the Allies would have to land at low tide in daylight, so that engineers could blast them out of the way. But he, too, thought that the Allies must seize a major port. This had never been the Allies intention. As early as June 1938, British Combined Operations planners had considered the idea of floating piers. General Dwight D. Eisenhower, who would become Supreme Commander of the invasion force and later president of the United States, recalled that when the idea of a floating harbour was first raised at a joint planning meeting in 1942 it was greeted with 'hoots and jeers' by the Americans. Despite this initial reaction, the Americans were won round and the floating harbour was to become a reality – though, admittedly, other methods were tried. There was a plan to build a breakwater by sinking old ships filled with concrete, until the boffins released the the sunken ships would have to be bigger than the supply ships that tied up against the breakwater. The size of the ships required to resupply the land forces meant that the ships sunk to make the breakwater would have to be bigger than any that were available. There were also experiments to create a 'calm area' where ships could be unloaded by creating a curtain of bubbles using compressed air. This was abandoned in favour of the Mulberry Harbour, which was tested successfully in Scotland in June 1943. Two were then built – one for the British sector and one for the American. They were designed to withstand gales of up to Force 6 on the Beaufort Scale, last for ninety days and deliver 12,000 tons of cargo to shore a day, whatever the weather. The American Mulberry failed to do this because it was put together in too much of a hurry, without proper soundings being taken, but it did well enough. Interrogation of captured German commanders after the invasion revealed that the Germans knew nothing of the Mulberry Harbours. This gave the Allies a huge advantage. Bringing their own harbours with them, meant that they could attack at any place along the coastline, giving them the element of surprise.

That vital operational plans, such as the deployment of the Mulberry Harbours were kept secret is tribute to the success of Operation Bodyguard. It was run by a secret office inside Churchill's headquarters called the London Controlling Section, under Colonel John Bevan and Lieutenant-Colonel Sir Ronald Wingate. They worked closely with 'C', the head of MI6; the counter-intelligence organisation MI5; and a special sector of MI5 called the XX ('Double-cross') Committee. The job of the XX Committee was to turn German agents. As all the German spies in Britain were picked up almost immediately, the XX Committee had plenty to chose from. Likely candidates were then subjected to lengthy interrogations by a special team in Battersea. To be a good spy, an individual needs to be resourceful and self-reliant, which implies a certain independence of mind. This meant that dedicated Nazis often did not make good spies. They were handed over to the civilian authorities for trial. Thirty of them were found guilty and executed. However, the XX Committee found that most of the agents recruited by the Abwehr, and not a few recruited by the SD, had grave misgivings about Nazism. After the German defeats at El Alamein and Stalingrad, it seemed Hitler was not so invincible after all and these agents became increasingly easy to turn. As double agents they were a potent weapon in feeding false information to Hitler. And as they were in contact with their handlers in Germany, the British knew what information was being requested. This gave them a powerful insight into the mind of the enemy.

The false information fed to German intelligence by double agents was backed by radio intercepts picked up the German Y Service, which tuned into all Allied radio traffic. Obviously, this had to be done subtly, with the utmost skill. If information came too easily, the enemy would smell a rat. Fortunately, Ultra told the Allies which of their codes the Germans had broken. These could be used to drop snippets of false information to the Germans which backed up what their agents were telling them. The Allies even used bursts of messages from a specific area, which the Y Service could identify with their direction-finding equipment, in codes the Germans had not broken to give the impression that there was a troop build-up there, as with the fictitious FUSAG, for example. Due to the differing frequency of traffic among the various tiers of an army – at corps, division and brigade levels – it was possible to create in the German mind an entirely fictitious order of battle. As the RAF controlled the skies over Britain, German reconnaissance aircraft were only allowed to see what the Allies wanted them to see. And German agents on the ground in Britain could confirm vital parts of the picture that German intelligence meticulously built up from the disinformation fed to them.

Newspapers were another important source of sending disinformation to the enemy as major British newspapers were often available in neutral countries. Clippings from the local press could also be sent via a neutral country to German spymasters. Provincial newspapers were a particularly good route to spread deception. They often included information about local men and women who were in the service, mentioning in passing their unit and their whereabouts. Engagements and marriages of service personnel filled the announcement columns and the letters pages carried complaints from local people protesting about the rowdy behaviour of men from a unit billeted in the area. By placing fictitious stories, personnel ads and letters according to a meticulous plan, a huge counterfeit canvas could be painted.

When America entered the war, the head of the FBI, J. Edgar Hoover, who was profoundly anti-British, would have nothing to do with the XX Committee. But after the establishment of the Office of Strategic Services, the forerunner of the CIA, under Major-General 'Wild Bill' Donovan in 1942, America set up the Joint Security Control (JSC), which mirrored the London Control Section, and Hoover created America's own XX Committee, known as X2. JSC and X2 ran a similar disinformation campaign in the US. During the planning of the Normandy invasion, the Anglo-American strategy of deception was co-ordinated by the Joint Committee of Special Means.

Even though J. Edgar Hoover had no time for the British, he was no slouch when it came to counter-intelligence. Even before America entered the war, he had a complete list of German agents working in the US (and a less complete one of the British agents operating there). Like the British, he was aided by the ineptitude of German intelligence. Agents were sent who had no real command of English. In one particularly inept operation, seven German agents were sent to sabotage American factories. On the way, they took leave in Paris. Their drunken conversations were overheard by the Resistance and details of their mission were passed on to MI6, who forwarded the information to the FBI. During this leave, one member of the party contracted a venereal disease and was unable to continue. On board the U-boat that was to land them surreptitiously on the eastern seaboard, they were given American money. This had been captured in the Pacific and some of it had been overprinted in Japanese. The rest was in old bills that were no longer legal tender. Once ashore, two of the German agents gave themselves up immediately and offered their services to the American government. Another, who was rather more dedicated, went into a drugstore to buy a razor and, through force of habit, clicked his heels, raised his arm in a Nazi salute and bellowed 'Heil Hitler!' He was promptly arrested.

However, not everything was plain sailing. After the fall of Canaris, suspicion fell on a British double agent, known as Artist, who was an Abwehr officer working out of Lisbon. He was kidnapped by the SD, drugged and smuggled back to Germany where he was interrogated by the Gestapo in the notorious Prinzalbrechtstrasse headquarters in Berlin. Artist had been recruited by a Yugloslav named Dusko Popov, a highly successful double agent who is believed to have been the model for James Bond. It has been alleged that Popov tried to deliver the plans for the attack on Pearl Harbor to, but Hoover, because of his hatred of the British, refused to accept them. If under torture, Artist blew Popov and the rest of his ring, the whole of Fortitude South would have been blown. Through Ultra, the Allies heard that Hitler had moved several reserve formations into Normandy. The D-Day planners held their breaths. But Artist did not talk. He either died under interrogation or was summarily executed and the all-important Fifteenth Army stayed east of the Seine.

As part of Fortitude North, the headquarters of a non-existent British Fourth Army was set up in Edinburgh, ready to decamp for Scandinavia at any time. In fact, the headquarters was just a handful of radio operators, sending out messages that the Germans would pick up. Others were deployed in Stirling and Dundee. Their radio traffic was so convincing that a German plane was sent to bomb the Dundee outpost. Meanwhile two German double agents, codenamed Mutt and Jeff, detailed the arrival of a Russian liaison officer. Part of the plan was for the Red Army to make a simultaneous thrust through Finland. He had been sent to co-ordinate the

Soviet part of the operation with the British Fourth Army and a small contingent of the fictitious American Fifteenth Army, stationed in Northern Ireland, that had also been earmarked for invasion of Norway.

Messages from this outfit gave the Germans the impression that it was a two-corps headquarters, with an armoured division, an airborne division and four infantry divisions. There were references to equipment and training in rock-climbing, skiing and other cold weather operations, along with details of sporting fixtures and social events.

As part of Fortitude North, Allied agents in Norway were asked for detailed information about the conditions and defences there. Even when this was done in codes that the Germans had not broken, the increase in radio traffic between Scotland and Norway convinced them that something was about to happen. Even the Soviets got in on the act, leaking disinformation about the mustering of an army ready for an assault on Scandinavia and naval preparations for an attack on the Finnish Arctic Sea port of Petsamo, then occupied by the Germans. Indeed, the Red Army really did attack Finland, a wartime ally of Germany, in June 1944 as part of their offensive in the east to coincide with the D-Day landings.

German intelligence naturally wanted confirmation that there was an army mustered in Scotland. They contacted their two most reliable agents in Britain: Dusko Popov, codenamed Tricycle, and a Spaniard known as Garbo. Both confirmed a military build up north of the border. Reconnaissance planes were sent over, which the RAF let through. They saw numerous planes on Scottish airfields – dummies made out of wood and canvas – and lochs full of Royal Navy warships. These were real, but they were not destined for Norway. They were part of Task Force 'S' which would head for Sword Beach in Normandy on D-Day.

To complete the picture, an Anglo-American military mission was sent to neutral Sweden to investigate the possibility of moving troops down to the Baltic. Air reconnaissance was increased. Commando raids along the Norwegian coast were stepped up. Factories, communication centres and railways were sabotaged. The volume of radio traffic to Norwegian and Danish resistance groups also grew. And shipping was attacked, resulting in fatal damage to the German battleship *Tirpitz* and the sinking of the troop ship *Donau* and a number of merchant vessels. The clinching piece of evidence, in the minds of German intelligence, was an entirely erroneous report of a visit of British Foreign Secretary Anthony Eden to Moscow, supposedly to conclude their plans to invade Scandinavia. Hitler became convinced that the Allies would attack in Norway and kept nearly half-a-million German troops, who could have been in France along with their artillery, tanks and air support, tied up in Norway for the rest of the war. When the Allies eventually turned up in Scandinavia, the war was over and 372,000 men surrendered with hardly a shot being fired.

Meanwhile the fictitious First US Army Group was mustering in south-east England ready for landings on the Pas de Calais. News of their existence was first supplied by the FBI though a triple agent, a Dutchman named Albert van Loop. A member of the Abwehr, he had been sent to Madrid where he approached the US Embassy and offered to work for the OSS or the FBI. To prove he was genuine he had handed over two ciphers, his call sign and various security checks. In fact, he was an Abwehr plant, though he had been told only to hand over one of his ciphers. The FBI were aware that he was still working for the Germans, but figured that he could be useful to them anyway. He was shipped to New York, where an American agent used the material he had provided to impersonate him. Information was then sent about real US Army units being shipped across the Atlantic for D-Day whose presence in England was bound to surface in the press anyway. Van Loop, unaware that he was being impersonated, also sent messages of his own, but due to the confusion surrounding the SD's takeover of the Abwehr, this did not alert anyone in Germany to the deception. When the FBI found that the Germans believed the impersonator, they began feeding them information about the FUSAG. In Britain, MI6's double agents and all the other methods perfected by London Controlling Section and the XX Committee were used to confirm its existence. The deception was so effective that Garbo was paid £20,000 by the Germans to run a non-existent spy ring dedicated to spying on the entirely non-existent FUSAG!

Garbo was a fanatical anti-Nazi, who had approached MI6 in Madrid early in the war. But he was a Spaniard and MI6 did not see what he could do for them. However, the Abwehr were willing to take him on. From Lisbon, using maps, newspapers and guide books, he began manufacturing fictitious reports from a non-existent network of three agents on his own account. When MI6 discovered that the German navy was combing the high seas for a non-existent convoy travelling from Liverpool to Malta that Garbo had made up, they recruited him and brought him to London where he expanded his network to fourteen non-existent agents. The Germans trusted him so much that they informed him every time the key of their Enigma traffic between Hamburg, Madrid and Tangiers was changed, saving Bletchley Park a great deal time working out the new key for themselves.

Another key agent in the disinformation campaign was Brutus, a Polish intelligence officer who had helped get the first Enigma machine to Britain before the war. When Poland was invaded, he escaped to Paris where he worked for MI6. He was betrayed to the Abwehr who were also on the lookout for enemy agents they could turn. He agreed to work for them, provide that the one hundred MI6 agents the Abwehr had already captured were treated as prisoners of war, rather than executed as spies. The Abwehr agreed and sent him to Madrid. From there he travelled to London where offered his services to MI6 once more. However, the XX Committee were reluctant to use him as the Abwehr knew that he had worked for MI6 before. Nevertheless they seemed to trust him, and he fed them information that he said he had gleaned in his new job as liaison officer between the RAF and the Polish Air Force.

A fourth agent used in Fortitude South was a Frenchwoman called Treasure. She had joined the Abwehr to get out of occupied France. They sent her to Britain, via Spain. In Madrid, she went to the British Embassy who took her to London where she was vetted by the XX Committee. She told the Abwehr that she had joined the Auxiliary Territorial Service, the women's wing of the British Army. Later she told her handlers that she had begun an affair in Bristol with an officer in the Fourteenth Army, part of FUSAG. When she reported that Fourteenth Army had been moved to Essex, ready for the invasion of the Pas de Calais, its presence there was verified by signal traffic intercepted by the German Y Service. Another clinching detail was that someone in Geneva began buying up all the Michelin maps of the Boulogne-Lille area. Hitler was all the more convinced that the main assault would come across the Straits of Dover when Y Service overheard that General George 'Old Blood and Guts' Patton had been appointed commander of the First Army Group.

The Luftwaffe increased its aerial reconnaissance over southeast England. They saw tracks indicating that tanks and other armoured vehicles were being hidden in the woods there. Other tanks were parked in plain sight. Landing craft were moored in the creeks and estuaries and, in Dover, what looked like a large oil refinery was being built to supply petrol to the invasion force. None of these was real. Special effects men and set builders had been recruited from theatres and movie studios to fool German air reconnaissance. They developed special track-making machines and made inflatable Sherman tanks, which looked like the real thing from the air. The landing craft were made out of plywood and canvas and the oil refinery in Dover was one huge movie set.

Although as far as the Germans were concerned, the First Army Group was under the command of Patton, the fictitious invasion of

the Pas de Calais was not going to be an exclusively American operation. The British Twenty-First Army under General Montgomery
was in on it too. His headquarters for the real invasion of Normandy
were in Portsmouth, but its radio traffic was relayed by land line to
a transmitter in Kent. So, in the build up to the real invasion, German
Y Service saw a dramatic increase in traffic from the very area an
invasion force heading for the Straits of Dover would muster.

Hitler fell for this hook, line and sinker, but Rommel was not so
sure. He had been pitted against Montgomery in the desert of North
Africa and knew his tactics. He suspected that the Allies were giving the impression that they had more divisions than they had. If
he was right, then there would only be one invasion, not three
spread across the Balkans, Norway and France. The build up of men
and materiel in England led him to believe that it would come in
France. To break through the Atlantic Wall, the Allies would have to
concentrate their forces on one small area to punch their way
through. In his inspection of the Atlantic Wall from Dunkirk to
Biarritz, the best place to attack was in Normandy. He figured that
the invasion would come just after daybreak, at low tide, preceded
by airborne landings. So he was prepared for landings on 5, 6 or 7
June, depending on the weather. But he could not shake from his
mind the idea that the Allies must take a port to succeed. Cherbourg
and Le Havre would be out of action by the time the invasion fleet
appeared over the horizon. And he wondered how the Allies would
give their landing force adequate air cover more than a hundred
miles from their air bases. Nevertheless, Rommel appealed to Hitler
to move four of his Panzer divisions to the west, ready for an attack
on the Normandy coast. Hitler refused. He remained convinced
that the invasion would come in the Pas de Calais. Besides, his
armoured reserves in the west were low due to Operation Zeppelin.
The Allied military planners followed the messages being sent back
and forth between Rommel and Hitler with interest via Ultra. They
learnt that, as a result of Hitler's intransigence, only two under-

strength, poorly equipped and thinly-spread divisions, with only horses and mules to move guns and supplies, were left to defend the Normandy beaches between Cherbourg and Le Havre.

Only one of the Allied deception operations seems to have failed. It was called Operation *Copperhead* and involved Montgomery's double, an actor named Clifton James. He appeared in Gibraltar, ostensibly to organise an invasion of the South of France. The Spanish dictator General Franco was also asked whether he would allow Barcelona to be used as the base for the evacuation and treatment of Allied wounded. This was naturally reported back to the Germans. Unfortunately, while Montgomery was a well-known teetotaller, James got very publicly drunk and the operation was cancelled. Ironically an Allied invasion of the South of France did take place. On 15 August 1944, the US Seventh Army and the French First Army landed on the Riviera, in Operation *Anvil* (later *Dragoon*). Operation Copperhead having failed to convince Hitler that a landing was planned in this area, there were only four German divisions to oppose them.

Although Rommel could not convince Hitler to move Panzers into Normandy, he directed his attention to strengthening the beach defences there. In May 1944, Allied air reconnaissance spotted a build up of the defences and obstacles along the Calvados coast. The German 6th Parachute Regiment was moved into the landing area and the 91st Air Landing Division, which specialised in anti-paratroop operations, moved into the Cherbourg peninsula and occupied areas that were going to be drop zones of the 82nd and 101st US Airborne divisions. These had to be moved but, as the timings of the drops had to mesh with the rest of the Overlord plan, they could not be moved far. Suddenly it seemed that Fortitude had been blown. In fact, Hitler had spotted that there was a weak point along the Normandy coast and had moved his troops to cover it. Maybe this was his much vaunted intuition coming into play. But still believing that the attack was coming in the Pas de Calais, he kept his Panzers to the east of the Seine.

Admiral Krancke, using his faulted analysis of the situation, calculated that the invasion would definitely come on 18 May. When it did not, he forecast that it would come in August. Meanwhile Von Rundstedt studied the pattern of Allied bombing in May. When he noticed that they were taking out the Seine bridges, he began to think that the Allies might make a landing in Normandy. But if they did land in Normandy, he believed that they would have to land on the Cherbourg peninsula itself because of their need for a port. Even then it would only be a minor or diversionary attack. He still agreed with Hitler that the Allied main force would land in the Pas de Calais.

Even though the Germans had strengthened their defences in Normandy, things were still looking very favourable for the Allies' landings there. Then, with just a week to go before D-Day, the Germans moved up the battle-hardened German 352nd Infantry Division. Direct from the Russian front, they would be responsible for the slaughter of American troops landing on Omaha Beach. The story is told that the Resistance group who reported their presence communicated with their British handlers via carrier pigeon and the pigeons carrying the message were shot as they passed over the coast. If this is true, the pigeon message was only a back-up. Information that 352nd Infantry were in Normandy did reach London, but the D-Day planners did not tell the men landing on Omaha Beach of their presence in case it had an adverse effect on morale.

In late May 1944, while troops of a dozen different nationalities disappeared from the pubs and shops of rural England and began mustering silently at the embarkation points, Operation Fortitude went into overtime. Radio traffic from Patton's fictitious First US Army Group was stepped up. While vehicles in full blackout moved to the embarkation ports, others with not-too-carefully hooded lights moved back and forth along the roads of south-eastern England. These movements were accompanied by a volley of reports from the XX Committee's double agents concerning troop movements in Kent and East Sussex. To add to the confusion, a new double agent, a young woman codenamed Bronx, told her German handlers that she had definite information that the landings would be in the Bay of Biscay on 15 June. Treasure then reported that she had made friends with the girlfriend of General Koenig of the Free French who had told her that the invasion would come on the Pas de Calais in the second week of July. In all, 250 messages were sent, each giving a different date and place for the invasion – including one from the French officer in Algiers saying that the invasion could come in Normandy on 5, 6 or 7 June. The officer may have been a triple agent working for the Germans, or London Controlling Section may have felt that if this possibility was overlooked, the Germans may draw their own conclusions. Sifting though the incoming messages, the new head of the SD, Walter Schellenberg, concluded that the French officer was right, the invasion would come in Normandy on 5, 6 or 7 June. But by that time the number of conflicting reports had left the reputation of German intelligence in tatters, and Schellenberg's conclusion led the German High Command to believe that the invasion would come anywhere but on the coast of Normandy, and on any day except 5, 6 or 7 June.

Admiral Krancke's belief that the invasion would definitely come on 18 May proved a godsend. Throughout May the weather was hot and dry and the sea was calm. It was perfect invasion weather and the German defenders grew tired of constant alerts, followed hours later by stand-downs. In Normandy the troops were doubly tired because of Rommel's ceaseless efforts to strengthen the defences there. By the first week of June everyone needed some sleep.

As sunny day followed sunny day and the Allies still did not come, scepticism spread. The defenders began to believe that the Allies were not going to invade at all. It had all been a huge ruse. The British and Americans were going to bid their time in England, safe on the other side of the Channel, and let the Russians do all the work – or postpone any invasion until the Germans were forced to take their troops away from the Atlantic Wall to defend the eastern border of the Fatherland.

With no sign of a seaborne landing coming across the Channel, there was a hiatus on the other fronts. In Italy, the Allies drew back from the fight as they prepared their push to link up with the Anzio beachhead and advance on Rome, while the Russians were preparing their summer offensive that was timed to coincide with the D-Day landings. Suddenly, in this quiet period, there were hundreds of commando raids knocking out German radar and radio-interception stations in Norway, Denmark, Rhodes, Crete, the Balkans and all over France. France itself seemed to be more dangerous than the Russian front as the Resistance began to take revenge on the occupiers. Factories and fuel-dumps blew up. Trains were derailed. And individual soldiers returning to their billets at night disappeared without trace. The German reaction was to slaughter any members of the Maquis they caught. Otherwise they took their revenge on innocent citizens. This provoked revulsion and hatred among the French people and the Resistance was soon recruiting more people than it lost.

Even Hitler began to think that the Allies' invasion preparations might all have been a hoax to distract his attention from the eastern front. Something had to be done to convince him that the attack across the Pas de Calais was about to go ahead; information about the imminent invasion must come from an unimpeachable source. It was decided that the former head of the Afrika Korps, Panzer General Hans Kramer, who held the Knight's Cross of the Iron Cross, with Oak Leaves, would be a suitable messenger. Since his capture in North Africa, Kramer had been held in a prisoner-of-war camp in South Wales, but he was in poor health and the Swedish Red Cross had organised his repatriation in May 1944. On his way out of the country, he was given a tour of ports full of shipping, airfields with their endless ranks of aeroplanes and bustling army assembly stations, and told that they were in Kent and East Sussex when they were, in fact, in Hampshire. The signposts had been removed from British roads in 1940 in the hope that it would disorientate invaders, so there was nothing to give the game away. Everything Kramer saw, apparently belonged to the First US Army Group. With the courtesy due to his rank as a general, Kramer was introduced to the commander-in-chief of FUSAG, General Patton himself. He also enjoyed an informal chat with Patton's senior officers who left him in no doubt that they were heading for Calais.

Kramer returned to Germany on the Swedish vessel *Gripsholm*, arriving on 23 May. His debrief once again convinced the Germans that the invasion was on. His reports of the Allied strength spread alarm and despondency. Göring even accused him of being a defeatist. The Germans went back on the alert once more. But they still had the same old problem. No one knew when or where the invasion would come – though Kramer had confirmed Hitler's view that the Pas de Calais was the place to watch.

It is not as if the Germans did not have their opportunities to find out the truth. Sergeant Thomas P. Kane, an American soldier of German descent in the Ordnance Supply Section of Supreme Headquarters in London, sent classified documents to his sister in Chicago by mistake. The authorities were alerted when the parcel burst open in an Illinois sorting office. Although the explanation was innocent enough, Kane, his sister and everyone in the sorting office who might have seen the documents were kept under strict surveillance until after D-Day.

Another breach of security came when a British staff officer left a briefcase containing the communication plan for Operation *Neptune*, the naval part of Overlord, in a taxi. Fortunately, the driver handed it in immediately at the Lost Property Office. At the beginning of June, an old army friend of General Eisenhower announced in the dining room of Claridges that the invasion would come before 15 June. He was demoted and sent back stateside.

Another American officer was also repatriated after getting drunk at a party and revealing top secret information.

But the worst scare came when eight tank landing craft were sunk by German E-boats while rehearsing for D-Day in Lyme Bay. Some 650 men were killed or drowned. Among them had been several 'Bigots' – the codename given to personnel who had been cleared to see invasion information at the highest level. Two of the E-boats had sailed slowly among the survivors and one of them was seen to switch on its searchlight as if looking for something. It was not beyond the bounds of possibility that prisoners had been taken. Divers were sent out to retrieve identity tags from the corpses. Eventually all the missing 'Bigots' were accounted for.

On the eve of D-Day, German signals intelligence worked out that all the RAF stations that were readying themselves for action were in south-west England, far from the Pas de Calais. This indicated that the attack would come in Normandy, but they could get no one in the High Command to listen to them. Hitler distrusted signals intelligence on principle. Their report merely led him to believe that a diversionary attack would be staged in Normandy. The level of radio traffic from FUSAG, which Kramer had now seen, convinced him that the attack was still coming across the Straits of Dover.

Nevertheless, as D-Day approached, the Allies were on tenterhooks. A senior British officer who did the Daily Telegraph crossword every morning discovered that Omaha and Utah, the codenames of two of the landing beaches in the US section, along with the words Overlord, Neptune and Mulberry came up in a series of five crosswords between 2 May and 2 June. Could undetected German spies be using the Telegraph crossword to send messages to Berlin? MI5 investigated. They discovered that the crosswords were compiled by two schoolmasters in Leatherhead, Surrey. The senior compiler had been doing the job for twenty years; the other was an old friend. Even though they had supplied the crosswords some six months in advance – before some of the codenames had even been thought up – they were subjected to the most stringent security checks and seemed genuinely distressed during their interrogation. The investigation gave them a clean bill of health, though the Americans were still sceptical.

Associated Press, in London's Fleet Street, actually announced the invasion on 3 June. A twenty-three-year-old teletype operator who had been working on a dry run for an invasion special accidentally ran the tape. News desks on five continents read the news:

URGENT PRESS ASSOCIATED NYK FLASH:
EISENHOWER'S HQ ANNOUNCES ALLIED LANDINGS IN FRANCE.

The mistake was rectified quickly enough to prevent the story being carried in any newspaper, but the news did reach both New York's Belmont Park racetrack and the Polo Grounds, where the New York Giants were playing the Pittsburgh Pirates. At both venues the crowds, at the announcers' request, rose to offer a silent prayer for the Allies' success.

General Eisenhower himself was considered a security risk because, with his wife back in America, he was having an affair with the ATS driver Kate Summersby, an Irish divorcee. This could have left him open to blackmail. Although Ireland was neutral during the war, and many men from the Republic fought valiantly for the Allies, many there harboured anti-British sentiments.

Churchill was another security risk as he spent a lot of time on the phone to Roosevelt. Ultra showed that the Germans were intercepting their calls and a new scrambler was installed in February 1944. However, from the length and frequency of the calls, Schellenberg somehow deduced that the invasion would come in France, not in the Balkans as Zeppelin implied.

The greatest invasion secret of all was the one hardest to conceal – the Mulberry Harbours. They were to be secured by huge concrete caissons, the size of apartment blocks. They were too big to be hidden or camouflaged and they were spotted moored off Tilbury by German reconnaissance planes. The Germans even seemed to know what they were for. On 21 April 1944, the radio propagandist William Joyce, known as Lord Haw-Haw for his sneering tone of voice, said, 'You think you are going to sink them on our coasts in the assault. We'll save you the trouble. When you come to get under way, we're going to sink them for you.'

As D-Day approached, fear spread though Supreme Headquarters. If the Germans were aware of the Mulberry Harbours, they would know that the Allies did not need to take a port with the first assault and there were few places along the coastline where floating harbours of sufficient scale could be deployed. Was it merely a coincidence that the Normandy beaches were being reinforced? Ultra came to the rescue again. The Japanese ambassador to Berlin, General Hiroshi Baron, sent regular reports back to Japan which were intercepted and decoded. The Allies found these very useful. In October 1943, Baron had toured the whole of the Atlantic Wall and sent a long, detailed report that was of more interest in Washington and London than it was in Tokyo. In April 1944, he toured the Wall again and was given a detailed briefing by General von Rundstedt. In it they discussed the huge caissons that the Luftwaffe had seen at Tilbury. Von Rundstedt had come to the conclusion that they were anti-aircraft gun towers. Hitler himself believed them to be replacements for harbour moles and jetties that might be destroyed by demolition charges or in an assault and this only strengthened his view that the Allies were going to seize a major port. So Bodyguard and the Mulberry secret were safe.

At the beginning of June, aerial bombardment of the inland targets began. But because the Germans were trying to install more V-1 launch ramps in the woods and forests of the Pas de Calais there was enough bombing in that area for the Germans to continue to believe that was where the assault would come. Meanwhile the defenders of the Atlantic Wall were complacent due to Krancke's statement that the invasion would not come now until August. The general feeling was that any attack would coincide with a Russian offensive. In the east, the thaw had come late that year and the Red Army would not be able to move until the end of June at the earliest. And when the weather began to change over France and the Channel, it was thought that the Allies had missed their chance. Even Krancke began to believe that the whole thing was a hoax and that Kramer had been deceived.

Rommel took the opportunity to brainstorm possible responses to an Allied landing. Once again he realised that it was vital that the Panzers were moved west of the Seine and put under his control. Once the Allies had gained a foothold, he believed, the only way they could be defeated was in a big set-piece battle which could only be won by a commander on the spot, not one hundreds of miles away in Rastenburg. Hitler had repeatedly refused to hand over command of the Panzers. Rommel began to believe that only way he could convince Hitler was if he went to see the Führer personally. Had the weather stayed fine, there was no way he could have left his headquarters in Normandy, but at the beginning of June it showed signs of breaking. Rommel's wife's birthday was on 5 June. He planned to pay a flying visit home, then go on to Hitler's headquarters where he had arranged a meeting with the Führer on 6 June. By then Rommel was the only senior officer who still believed that the invasion was coming. But that only led him to make another major mistake. Fearing air raids, Rommel had removed the guns from their emplacement in many places along the Wall. During his assessment of the Wall, he had noted that they lacked the necessary thirteen feet of concrete to protect them from bombing. The guns would be safe enough if they were kept nearby, well-camouflaged. He believed that he would have at least twenty-four hours' warning of any attack, which would give his men plenty of time to put them back. But the defenders in Normandy did not get twenty-four hours warnings of the invasion, and when it came Rommel was not even in France to order the guns' return.

On 1 June a storm began to blow up. Nevertheless Eisenhower set the date for the invasion as 5 June. The forecasts got worse and, by 3 June, he postponed it until 6 June. One convoy of 140 ships, carrying the US 4th Infantry Division, was already on its way and out of radio contract. If they arrived at the beaches alone, without support, there would be a massacre. A plane was sent which dropped a canister containing a message telling them to turn back. It fell in the sea. The pilot scrawled a second message, put it in another canister and, this time, managed to hit the deck of the commodore's ship. After what seemed like hours, the convoy turned back towards the English coast.

Everything now depended on the weather. At a pinch, they could delay until 7 June. Otherwise, they would have to wait fourteen days until the tides were right again. Men and equipment were now aboard the invasion fleet. They would have to disembark, return to their assembly areas and go through the whole embarkation procedure again two weeks later. This, it was thought, would have a disastrous effect on morale.

Then on 4 June, Eisenhower's chief meteorologist Group Captain John Stagg spotted a lull in the storm. Between the afternoons of Monday 5 June and Tuesday 6 June the weather would be calm enough for Operation Neptune to go ahead. It was a huge risk. Weather forecasts are never that accurate. The air chiefs, Air Chief Marshal Sir Trafford Leigh-Mallory and Air Chief Marshal Sir Arthur Tedder, were worried about the flying conditions. But Eisenhower and Montgomery were both ready to take a chance. They knew that bad weather would only add to the element of surprise. No one would expect the Allies to invade during a storm. They knew the Germans would know nothing of the lull in the storm that was approaching. The Allies had gone to great lengths in tracking down and destroying or jamming all the enemy's weather ships.

As the invasion plan got under way, Allied airstrikes turned from targets inland to the coastal defences. German-occupied ports were mined and there was an increase in the coded messages being sent to the French Resistance on the BBC. But still the Germans thought it was a hoax and air reconnaissance revealed no build up of landing craft in Dover harbour. As the weather closed, in patrols by German reconnaissance aircraft, E-boats and submarines were cancelled. The Germans were convinced that the weather made an invasion impossible.

To keep the Germans in the dark, the Resistance began cutting all telephone and telegraph wires, while three-man teams were airdropped in to organise special operations. One group was captured and gave away the signal that would alert the Resistance that the invasion was on the way. The signal was a line from the poem 'Chanson d'Autome' by Paul Verlaine. But when the line was broadcast repeatedly by the BBC, it was dismissed because of the bad weather. Later the defenders manning the Atlantic Wall in the Pas de Calais went on the alert, while those in Normandy took leave, attended parties, wrote letters home, or simply slept.

On the night of 5–6 June, as Operation Neptune went into action, all Allied intelligence could to do was monitor German radio traffic. Ultra picked up nothing untoward and, as far as anyone could tell, the Germans had no idea of what was about to happen. Meanwhile one final pre-D-Day piece of deception was going into action. Lancaster bombers dropped chaff – strips of radar-reflecting metal – at precise intervals across the Straits of Dover. They also used an electronic device called Moonshine which give enemy radar operators multiple images of a plane, making a handful of aircraft look like a huge squadron. Then launches towing barrage balloons carrying radar reflectors set out into the pitching sea. Soon radar operators on the Pas de Calais saw what appeared to be a huge fleet covering an area of some two hundred square miles coming their way. While in Normandy there was no alert and no German gun fired until the invasion fleet appeared over the horizon, in the

Straits of Dover searchlights swept the waters, coastal batteries opened fire and naval units put to sea to find – nothing at all. Then just a few minutes after midnight on 6 June – D-Day itself – hundreds of dummy paratroopers were dropped. When they hit the ground they set off detonators which simulated the sound of small arms fire. Flares, smoke canisters, mortar bombs and machine-gun simulators were also dropped. These were aimed at woods where it would be difficult to know what was going on. But it appear that a full-scale airborne assault was in progress and battle was raging on the ground. These dummy assaults even drew some of the defenders of Omaha Beach away from their positions, which meant the slaughter there was not quite as bad as it might have been.

The assault troops were now on their way. With them they carried detailed maps of what confronted them. Eisenhower said that it was unlikely that any army had ever gone into battle better informed. The Allied intelligence gathering operation had been a complete triumph. So had their deception plan, which continued after the landings. Hitler held back his Fifteenth Army in the Pas de Calais, awaiting the non-existent First US Army Group until long after the Allies had broken out of their beachhead. Hitler himself, it has been said, was the most valuable weapon in the Allied armoury. Believing himself to be a military genius, he stayed away from the battle front, directing the fighting from his Wolf's Lair where he could be deceived by tricks as old as war itself.

4

THE ALLIED FORCES

THANKS TO THE SUCCESS of the Allied deception operations, the landing forces would at least have the element of surprise, but generally history was against them. The ANZACs' amphibious landing at Gallipoli in the First World War had been a failure. The Canadians had done little better at Dieppe in 1942. There had been successful amphibious assaults in North Africa in 1942 and in Sicily and Salerno in 1943. But these had not been against fortified coastlines. In North Africa, Allied forces had been pitted against a French colonial army and achieved surprise by neglecting to make a formal declaration of war. Even then they ran into difficulties. At Sicily, dispirited Italian troops put up little resistance, but even there, there were self-inflicted casualties. Allied troop planes carrying the US 82nd Airborne Division had been shot down by Allied naval gunfire, and at Salerno, the Germans had almost succeeded in forcing the Allies back into the sea.

Despite the manifest dangers of launching an all-out attack on a heavily fortified shore, the invasion had its own momentum. The British had managed to talk the Americans out of a cross-Channel assault in 1942 and 1943, but chairman of the joint chiefs of staff General George C. Marshall had built the US Army up from 170,000 in 1940 to 7.2 million three years later and he was not prepared to see them squandered in a small theatre of war such as Italy. The British faced the constant threat that, if these men were not committed to an invasion of France, they would be sent to fight in the Pacific. Although Churchill, particularly, was nervous about an assault on France, he had always known it had to be done. As early as 1940, he told the head of combined operations, Lord Louis

Mountbatten, 'You are to prepare for the invasion of Europe, for unless we can go and land and fight Hitler and beat his forces on land, we shall never win this war.'

There were the politics of the situation to consider as well. Until the Allies were on the beaches of France, the situation on the Eastern Front was always liable to change. Firstly, there was the possibility that Hitler and Stalin would sign a separate armistice in the east. Secondly, Hitler may decide to throw his entire force against the Soviets and force the Red Army back; thirdly, the Soviets would beat Hitler single-handedly and occupy the whole of western Europe. Until the Second World War, Churchill had always been a staunch anti-Communist. He had supported the Allied intervention into Russia in 1919 in an attempt to strangle the Soviet state at birth. When asked how he could make an alliance with Stalin during World War II, he said he would make a pact with the devil if Hell would fight Hitler.

Even though Hitler's boast that he had created Fortress Europe was a little overblown, the Germans had a strong hand. They had huge, well-designed fortifications, good communications on secure land lines and they would be fighting on the defensive. However, the Allies had a few things in their favour too, particularly the control of the sea and air. They could also pick the time and place where the assault would occur. But as soon as the invasion began, the advantage switched back to the Germans. Until the beachhead was big enough to get half-tracks ashore, the landing forces would only be able to move as fast as their legs could carry them. The Germans would be able to move their reinforcements speedily by road and rail. It would also be easy to supply them, while every bullet, every bandage, every K ration the Allies used would have to be brought across the Channel.

The landing forces would also be vastly outnumbered. The Germans had fifty infantry divisions and eleven armoured divisions in France in 1944. At most, the Allies would be able to land five divisions on the first day and it would take up to seven weeks to land the forty divisions that had been mustered in England. A counter-attack would begin in the first week. However, if that could be resisted, the build up of the massive amounts of arms and materiel coming out of US factories would win through in the end. The US military doctrine was that wars were won by organisation and administration. The best men went to the rear-area positions where they controlled the management of the war and the flow of men and materiel. The less good went to the fighting arms and the worst went into the infantry. But if the frontline troops got the ammunition and equipment they needed when they needed it, victory was assured. It was accepted that losses were going to be substantial.

Although the Wehrmacht had achieved its aims in 1939 and 1940 by outflanking and outmanoeuvring its opponents, by 1944 the war had reverted to the First World War model. The Red Army made massive frontal assaults that were costly for both sides. And in the narrow Italian peninsula, there was no room for outflanking movements. The Allied push had become a war of attrition. It would be the same in Normandy, initially. A landing on a beach on a forti-fied coastline was, by its very nature, a frontal assault.

In the First World War, attacking armies softened up the defences by massive artillery bombardment. In Normandy this would be supplied by the enormous British and US fleets in the Channel. However, it was decided that the element of surprise was more important so the pre-landing bombardment was limited to half an hour.

Next there was the problem of landing men and machines on the enemy shore. The Germans had prepared for their planned inva-sion of Britain in 1940 by mustering barges from Europe's canals and rivers. These would have been towed across the Channel filled with troops. But with flat-bottomed barges, this could only have been done in a flat calm. However, the Americans had already put their mind to this, even before the war.

Anticipating a war against Japan in the late 1930s, the US Marines had experimented with landing craft to make amphibious assaults on island beaches. In 1941, the British took up the idea with the landing ship, tank (LST) and the landing craft, tank (LCT). The LST was a large vessel as big as a light cruiser. It was 327 feet long and displaced 4,000 tons. Flat-bottomed, it would be difficult to handle in high seas, but it could be beached. Doors in the bow would then swing aside, a ramp would be lowered and dozens of tanks and trucks would drive ashore from its cavernous hold. It could also carry small landing craft on its deck.

The LCT was smaller, 110 feet long, and could carry between four and eight tanks, which would be landed via a ramp. Although, again, it was flat-bottomed, it was more stable than the LST, and could handle rough seas. When the US came into the war, they took over the production of LSTs and LCTs.

By D-Day, they had already been tested successfully in the Mediterranean. But they had their shortcomings. They were slow, hard to manoeuvre and made easy targets. The grim joke among landing forces was that LST stood for Long Slow Target. Nevertheless they became the workhorse of Allied amphibious operations.

LSTs and LCTs were good for bringing armour ashore, but they were no good for putting ashore the men needed in the initial assault. What was needed was a smaller boat that could be beached, extract itself, turn around without being turned over by the waves and go back to the mother ship to pick up more men. Again, it would need a front ramp so that the assault force could attack the beach in a rush. Climbing over the side would mean that the invaders would be attacking singly and be easy to pick off.

There were numerous different designs because their construction was put out to small shipbuilders who each made their own version. At the time American navy yards were tied up with making the Liberty ships that carried cargo across the Atlantic and their escort vessels. They took all the steel and marine engines available.

Building a fleet of landing craft big enough to carry three to five divisions across the Channel in one day taxed even the might of American industrial production.

'The destinies of two great empires seemed to be tied up in some goddamned things called LSTs,' rued Churchill.

The man who solved the problem was a hard-drinking Irishman named Jack Higgins. A self-taught New Orleans boat designer, he had built boats for the oil companies who were exploring the bayous of southern Louisiana in the 1930s. They had needed a boat that could run up onto the bank, then be refloated with the minimum of trouble. He built the 'Eureka' boat, made of wood, that did the job.

In the late 1930s, Higgins realised that war was coming and there would be an enormous demand for small boat. He also saw that there would be a shortage of steel so, in 1939, he bought up the entire Philippines crop of mahogany. The initial demand for landing craft came from the Marines. The US Navy had no interest in landing craft. They liked big ships, so they put the design out to competition. Higgins won with his design for the diesel-powered landing craft, vehicle and personnel (LCVP) based on his Eureka design. It also became known as the Higgins boat. Although the Navy bureaucrats hated working with the hard-drinking Higgins, the Marines loved his craft. Thirty-six feet long and ten-and-a-half feet wide, it could carry a platoon of thirty-six men, or a jeep and a squad of twelve. The ramp was metal but the rest of it was made out of plywood. In even a moderate sea, waves would break over the bow and sides, but it could land men on a beach in a matter of seconds, before turning out into the open water.

Higgins set up small production lines all over New Orleans. Unusually for the time, he employed both women and African-Americans, paying top dollar regardless of sex or race. At the peak of production he employed 30,000 workers. They produced more than 20,000 LCVPs, along with hundreds of LCTs, improved by his own design, and dozens of PT patrol boats which, again, he designed.

Higgins boats were brought across the Atlantic, and later across the Channel, on the deck of LSTs. They saw action in the Mediterranean, Normandy and the Pacific and landed more American fighting men than all other types of landing craft put together.

'He was the man who won the war for us,' Eisenhower once said.

Other small producers came up with the landing craft, medium (LCM), and the landing craft, infantry (LCI). The LCI was 160 feet long and carried two hundred men that were discharged down ramps either side of the bow. Then there was the DUKW, or 'Duck'. This was a standard US two-and-a-half-ton truck fitted with floatation tanks and propellers. It could make five-and-a-half knots in a moderate sea and fifty miles an hour on land.

On D-Day, the Allies would not just be landed from the sea. They would also arrive from the air. Although the Germans had pioneered the use of paratroopers in the invasion of Holland, they had abandoned airborne operations after massive losses during the invasion of Crete. Besides, by 1944, they did not have the aircraft to deploy them. But the Allies had no shortage of planes, and paratroopers were dropped by the Allies' airborne workhorse, the Dakota, made by Douglas Aircraft. The company had adapted its twin-engined civilian airliner, the DC-3, which was redesignated the C-47 for military use. It was unarmed, unarmoured and slow, but it was dependable, versatile and could drop a stick of eighteen paratroopers accurately over a target. The British had two airborne divisions, the 1st and the 6th, and the Americans had the 82nd and the 101st. These elite forces were made up of volunteers. The troops landed by glider and the rest of the infantry were largely conscripts.

While the British were running short of manpower, the US Army had no shortage of recruits. They rejected one-third of the men that were called up after an initial examination. As a result the average American soldier was taller, heavier and healthier than their enemy counterpart. They were also brighter. Nearly half the enlisted men had graduated from high school and one in ten had been to college.

Their average age was twenty-six.

They may have been the best-educated army ever to go to war, but they were also the greenest. Only two of the fifty American divisions that were selected to serve in north-west Europe had seen action before: the 1st Infantry and the 82nd Airborne. Although Britain had been at war for four years, very few British troops had been in action either. None of the units designated for the D-Day landings had more than a handful of veterans. This was not necessarily a bad thing: in a direct assault on a well-fortified position, men who have not seen what a bullet, a land mine or a mortar round can do to the human body have a great advantage.

'A veteran infantryman is a terrified infantryman,' said US Ranger Carl Weast, who landed on D-Day. And Carwood Lipton, a sergeant in the 101st Airborne admitted, 'I took chances on D-Day I would never have taken later in the war.'

Young men in their late teens and early twenties have a sense of invulnerability. When told by an officer on the eve of D-Day that nine out of ten men would become casualties, Private Charles East of 29th Infantry Division looked at the men around him and said to himself, 'You poor bastards.'

However, morale among the American troops mustered for D-Day was not high. After just eight months, casualties in Italy had reached 150,000 and losses on the Normandy beaches were expected to be much higher. US troops adopted an attitude of fatalism, and soldiers who think they are going to be killed often lack the fighting spirit.

Montgomery had carefully sprinkled veterans from his Eighth Army, which had seen action in North Africa and Italy, throughout other units. They were living proof that you could survive and calmed the fears of the younger troops. The British and Canadians were also keen to avenge Dunkirk and Dieppe. This gave them well-defined incentives that the Americans lacked. On the other hand, the British lacked the aggressive instinct that can be instilled by the brutal discipline of a totalitarian state and the British War Office were afraid to impose strict discipline on a democratic army in case in dampened their fighting spirit.

'The trouble with our British lads is that they are not killers by nature,' wrote General Montgomery. And the Americans complained that the British were always stopping to make tea.

There were other tensions between the Allies. As the British had been fighting over two years longer than the Americans, they adopted an attitude of superiority. They saw the Americans as under-prepared and, essentially, civilians in uniform. There was some truth to this. General Maxwell Taylor, wartime commander of the 101st Airborne, boasted that, by December 1944, some of the companies in his division were better than anything anywhere. But, he admitted, 'it did take some time.'

The British, by contrast, had more of a military culture. Many of their officers had fought in the First World War. Although the British Army had been greatly expanded, it maintained its old regimental system. Many of the American units had been started from scratch, and while GIs were enjoying a final leave before D-Day, the British were training up to the last minute.

The Americans considered the British overcautious. They believed the war could only be won by taking risks. Again there is some truth in this. But Britain was running low on manpower and could not risk large losses, while the huge reserves of recruits in the US had only begun to be tapped. Commanders such as General Montgomery had seen the slaughter of the First World War and would not commit their men to battle unless they vastly outnumbered the enemy.

But despite the tension between the Allies, there was also a mutual respect. It has been said, with some justification, that the war in the west was won by a marriage between American brawn and British brains. America had the manpower and the spare industrial capacity. In 1939, American factories were running at half their capacity and only 800 military planes were made that year. When President Roosevelt called for production to be raised to 4,000 a month, everyone thought he was crazy. But by 1942 America was indeed producing 4,000 planes a month and by 1943 this figure had risen to 8,000.

But it was the British who had broken the Enigma code though and, through their Double Cross system, kept the Germans believing throughout the war that their code was unbreakable and their secrets were safe. The British came up with the Mulberry Harbour – without it, any invasion would almost certainly have failed – and PLUTO, the undersea pipeline that pumped petrol across the Channel, which saved carrying it in vulnerable tankers. The British had developed radar, the proximity fuse, and Hobart's Funnies, a number of devices designed to breach the concrete emplacements and the minefields of the Atlantic Wall. They were the brainchildren of General Percy Hobart. He developed the Crab tank, a tank fitted with a rotating drum at the front that flailed the ground with chains to detonate mines, the AVRE (Assault Vehicle Royal Engineers) tank that could carry a forty-foot box girder bridge to cross anti-tank ditches and the swimming tank, the DD or Duplex Drive tank. This had an inflatable canvas screen, which allowed the tanks to float, and propellers which ran from its engine. Hobart's amphibious tanks were designed to swim ashore in front of the landing crafts, assault (LCAs) to give cover to the infantry. The British had also done much of the preliminary work on the atomic bomb before the Americans came into the war and had developed penicillin which saved thousands of lives on the battlefield.

Although General Eisenhower was to be supreme commander – for political reasons the top job had to go to an American – General Montgomery was to have overall command on land of the invasion force on land, Admiral Sir Bertram Ramsay at sea and Air Chief Marshal Sir Trafford Leigh-Mallory in the air. And a fourth British officer, Air Chief Marshal Sir Arthur Tedder, was to be deputy supreme commander. When Montgomery was appointed to command the invasion on New Year's Day 1944, he threw away the invasion plan that the Americans had been working on since 1942. He considered that the assault force in the American plan would not be powerful enough to do the job and the attack was on too narrow a front. He insisted on upping the number of landing divisions from three to five and the number of airborne divisions from one to three. Montgomery presented his own plan to the military commanders and senior politicians at St Paul's School in West Kensington on 15 May 1944. It was accepted. A key part of the plan was that, on D-Day itself, there would be an equal number of British and American troops. But, as losses mounted, the British would not be able to sustain that commitment. Eventually, the war in western Europe would become a predominantly American affair. To reflect this, Eisenhower himself would take over command of the land forces.

While the invasion plan was being prepared, the military build-up was already underway. By the spring of 1944, the whole of southern England had become one vast military encampment. Under trees at the sides of roads, protected by corrugated iron, were dumps of ammunition and engineering stores. Fields were full of Sherman tanks, Dodge trucks, jeeps and field guns. There were row after row of them that reached to the horizon.

The fleet, comprising 138 battleships, cruisers and destroyers, was assembled to bombard the French coast. These were accompanied by 279 escorts, 287 minesweepers, 4 line-layers, 2 submarines, 495 motor boats, 310 landing ships and 3,817 landing craft and barges for the initial assault. Another 190 LCVPs and 220 LCTs would join them as part of the ferry service to get more personnel and equipment ashore after the beachhead had been secured. Another 423 ships, including tugs, would be involved in the construction of the Mulberry Harbours and the laying of the PLUTO pipeline that would pump petrol ashore and telephone cables connecting the commanders on the ground to SHAEF (Supreme

Headquarters, Allied Expeditionary Force) in London. A further 1,260 merchant ships would also be involved, making a total of over 7,000 vessels.

It was, of course, impossible to keep such a huge build-up secret, but if the deception that this force was to be thrown against the Pas de Calais was to be maintained the enemy's access to information must be limited. Visitors were banned from a corridor extending ten miles inland from the coast. Civilian travel between Britain and Ireland was banned to prevent contact between enemy agents and the German Embassy in Dublin. All movement of foreign diplomats in and out of the UK was prohibited, and the eighty press correspondents who were to accompany the invasion force were rounded up on 22 May and kept incommunicado until the troops were ashore.

Some 10,000 aircraft were also deployed in Operation Overlord. They would bomb key targets, drop paratroopers, tow gliders carry airborne troops and protect the airspace above the assault force. In all more than six million people were involved in the D-Day landings. Twenty US divisions, fourteen British, three Canadian, one French and one Polish division were billeted in southern England, along with hundreds of thousands of other troops belonging to special forces, headquarters units, communication staff, and corps personnel. Then suddenly, as this huge force made its way to the embarkation ports, silently at night, these men simply disappeared.

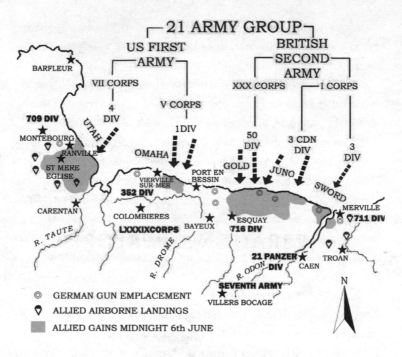

The Normandy beaches
6 June 1944

PART TWO
OPERATION OVERLORD

5

THE AIRBORNE ASSAULTS

THE USE OF AIRBORNE TROOPS was a rather late addition to the D-Day plan. General Omar N. Bradley, commander of the American landing forces, was the only senior commander who favoured their use. He proposed dropping the 82nd 'All American' and the 101st 'Screaming Eagles' behind the Atlantic Wall to seize the causeways that ran inland from the American beaches, and cut off the Cotentin Peninsula to prevent the Germans reinforcing Cherbourg. Air Marshal Leigh-Mallory was against it and Montgomery only agreed if Bradley took full responsibility for the operation. Bradley agreed.

The British caution was natural. The use of airborne troops was relatively new and did not have a good track record, although it had started out well enough. On 10 May 1940, a German paratroop regiment had seized Holland in a single day, and in April and May 1941, the German airborne assault on the island of Crete took the island in just eight days. During that operation, forty-six RAF planes were lost and 12,000 British prisoners of war were taken. However, the Germans lost between 4,500 and 6,000 men and between 271 and 400 aircraft. The loss of so many of his elite paratroopers so appalled Hitler that he forbade future large-scale paratroop operations and, for the Germans at least, the day of the paratrooper was over.

However, the Allies did not know the extent of the German losses on Crete and continued planning paratroop operations of their own. These had begun on 22 June 1940, when Churchill had ordered the formation of a corps of airborne troops within forty-eight hours. He envisaged an initial force of 5,000. They were to be trained that summer. Their first action was on 10 February 1941, when thirty-five of them were dropped in Southern Italy to destroy the Monte

Vulture aqueduct which supplied the towns of Brindisi, Bari and Foggia where there were dockyards and military installations. Then on 12 November 1942, the 3rd Battalion of Britain's 1st Parachute Brigade captured the Bône airfield in North Africa after being dropped by USAAF C-47s.

On 16 August 1942, the US 82nd and 101st Airborne Divisions were officially activated. They comprised 17,650 'lean and mean' volunteers, some of whom did not survive their rigorous and dangerous training. The first mass airborne drop of Allied troops occurred over Sicily on 10 July 1943. Four hours after the jump, Colonel James M. Gavin, commander of the 82nd Airborne, could only muster twenty men out of the 3,400 that had boarded planes in North Africa. Some of the troops landed sixty miles east of the drop zone. The British fared little better. Only fifty-seven out of their 156 planes dropped their troops anywhere near the target. In all, 605 officers and men were lost, including 326 who landed in the sea and were drowned. Eisenhower wrote to Marshall in Washington, telling him that he had no faith in airborne troops as, once the force had been scattered, he doubted that it could ever be melded back into an effective fighting unit.

Marshall disagreed and, at one point, suggested that the invasion of Normandy should be primarily an airborne assault, with the landings on the beaches as subsidiary action. Eisenhower rejected this out of hand, but slowly became convinced that an airborne operation might make a decisive difference on the Cotentin Peninsula and in the battle for Cherbourg. Later a British airborne landing to the east of the beaches was planned to protect the flank and continue the deception that the invasion would take place on the Pas de Calais.

The Americans were unlucky in their choice of drop zones. Utah Beach was at the base of the Cotentin Peninsula. Behind it run the Merderet and Douve rivers. Napoleon's engineers had devised a series of canals and ditches there which the Germans used to flood the area. The 101st Airborne under Major-General Maxwell D. Taylor had to seize the roadways and causeways that ran through these flooded fields so that the landing force could escape from the beach. The 82nd Airborne under Major-General Matthew B. Ridgeway were to land at the Merderet River, west of the village of St Mère-Église and seize the village and the crossroads there to prevent the Germans counter-attacking from the north-west. Fortunately, the Germans were not expecting the Allies to land there. They had laid out their defensive formations and their *Rommelspargel* or 'Rommel's asparagus' – sharpened poles that were deadly both to paratroopers and gliders trying to land – further to the rear.

At 0100 hours on 6 June 1944, the Pathfinders went in. These were an advance force who were to mark the drop zones with radio direction finder beacons and lights in large 'T' shapes on the ground. But there were problems. A cloud bank over the coast forced the Dakotas carrying them to climb above it or drop below it. This meant that the Pathfinders jumped from too high or too low an altitude. Anti-aircraft fire also forced the pilots to take evasive action, throwing them off course. One Pathfinder team landed in the Channel and only one, out of eighteen, landed where it was supposed to.

Half an hour later, and five hours before men hit the beaches, the Germans saw the 925 C-47s of the United States IX Air Force Troop Carrier Command fly over and six regiments – some 13,400 men in all – descend from the skies. Again there were problems. For most of the pilots, it was their first combat mission and they had not been trained for night flying, bad weather flying, or flak-avoidance. They flew in groups of nine, separated from the planes on each side by just 100 feet – a C-47 measured 95 feet from wing-tip to wing-tip. Each group was separated by just 1,000 yards from the groups before and aft. They flew without navigation lights and all they could see of the plane ahead was a tiny blue dot on the tail.

They crossed the Channel at 500 feet to avoid detection by German radar, following a course sent up a radio beacon carried by a British patrol boat and a light carried by a British submarine. Over the Channel Islands, they climbed to 1,500 feet to avoid anti-aircraft fire. The batteries on the Channel Islands opened up, but their only effect was to wake the American paratroopers who had been knocked out by the anti-airsickness pills they had been issued. Over the coast they were to descend again to 600 feet: the jump height was set low so that the paratroopers would spend less time in their vulnerable descent. But as they crossed the coastline, they too ran into the cloud bank. The planes automatically dispersed to avoid the danger of mid-air collision. When they emerged, some found they were alone.

It was then that all hell broke loose. Search lights and tracers raked the skies. The Dakotas were hit by 88mm shells, 20mm shells and machine-gun fire. Some planes exploded, others plunged towards the ground. The pilots had been instructed to slow down to 90 mph for the drop, to minimise the shock to the jumpers. But a plane flying at 600 feet and 90 mph is a sitting duck, so the pilots threw the throttle forward until they were doing 150 mph. They had no real idea where they were, except that they were somewhere over the Cotentin Peninsula. The pilots wanted to get out of it, and flicked on the red light, telling the paratroopers to stand up and hook up, as they passed over the Channel Islands. At the first possible opportunity, the pilots then flicked the light to green, hoping to get rid of their charges and return to England as fast as possible. The men then made the $10,000 jump – it was called the $10,000 jump as GIs were required to take out a $10,000 life assurance policy to provide for their families in the event of their death. As they jumped, many saw planes below them. Some planes got hit by equipment dropped from above them. One paratrooper got caught on the wing of a plane below.

Some men had already been wounded by shrapnel inside the

plane. Others refused to jump when they saw the fireworks out-side. Those who did jump found themselves either too low or too high. And they were sitting ducks as flares lit up the night sky. The Germans even set fire to a hay barn, so they could pick off the US paratroopers as they came down. Those who made it to the ground found the situation confused to say the least. Men from the 82nd Airborne found themselves in the 101st's drop zone and vice versa. In the dark, they were supposed to identify each other by the metal-lic toys that made the click of a cricket. Unfortunately, this was hard to distinguish from the sound of a safety catch being taken off.

General Taylor, of the 101st, found himself completely alone. After twenty minutes, he hooked up with a private and a lieutenant, his aide. They tried to find out where they were with a map and a flashlight, but between the three of them they came to three differ-ent conclusions. More men turned up. Soon Taylor had gathered a group consisting of two generals, four colonels, four lieutenants, a handful of NCOs and a dozen privates. 'Never have so few been commanded by so many,' Taylor commented sardonically.

But Taylor and his men were lucky. Some landed in areas that the main force would not reach until twenty-five days later. Lieutenant-Colonel Louis Mendez walked for five days, covering ninety miles, without encountering another American, though he managed to managed to kill six Germans on the way. Some fell in the Channel, while others were captured as soon as they landed.

Rommel had ordered the lock gates on the Merderet River opened at high tide and closed at low tide, so the area where the 82nd Airborne were to land was flooded. This had not shown up on aerial reconnaissance. Although the water was only a metre deep, it was enough to drown a fully-laden paratrooper or one who could not detach his chute fast enough. The British had a quick-release device on their harnesses, but the Americans had fiddly buckles on theirs. Thirty-six troops of the 82nd drowned that night. A com-plete stick – that is, the squad of men who jump from one plane –

went missing. One hundred and seventy-three men had broken an arm or a leg, and sixty-three had been taken prisoner.

Only four per cent of the 82nd landed in their target zone to the west of the Merderet river. Three days later, the 82nd was still at one-third strength and 4,000 men were missing. This meant they could not secure all the causeways across the Merderet and Douve rivers. The 101st were even worse off. They could only muster 1,000 out of their 6,000 men.

General James Gavin was in command of the men who were supposed to take St Mère-Église. Over the Channel he had kept a watchful eye on the twenty planes in his formation. But by the time his plane had emerged from the clouds and the green light came on, he could only see two others. It took him almost an hour to find the twenty men who jumped with him. He only discovered where he was when a patrol he had sent out found a railway line. More patrols managed to muster 150 men, but none of them was armed with anything heavier than a rifle or carbine. Heavy equipment seems to have landed in the flooded fields and disappeared under the water. Stragglers informed him that there were other Americans on the other side of a bridge at the village of La Fière which was one of the division's objectives. Gavin headed there, but he found his way barred by German armour that held the bridge. There was a stand-off. Without anti-tank weapons they could not dislodge the Germans and join up with the rest of the division, while the Germans were heavily outnumbered and could make no headway. The stand-off was only broken four days later when American armour arrived from the beachhead.

The 506th Regiment landed near the target of St Mère-Église, but had scattered, while the 505th had the misfortune of landing on the village itself. They were shot as they fell from the sky – the Germans had a machine-gun in the bell tower of the church. One shot hit a man's grenades and an empty chute was left floating to the ground. Another man was sucked into a house that was on fire.

Men were shot down when they landed in the village square or left hanging from trees or telegraph poles. But some made it to the ground safely and managed to take revenge on the Germans. In the one success of the night, 1,000 troops mustered outside St Mère Église, out of the 2,200 that were supposed to be there. By dawn it was the first town in France to be liberated and the Stars and Stripes hung outside the town hall where the Nazi swastika had hung for four years. Unfortunately that was only the beginning of the town's troubles. The Germans shelled St Mère Église for the next two days, flattening many of the buildings and killing dozens of the inhabitants. The first US casualty report came from St Mère-Église. It listed 756 missing, 347 wounded and 156 dead.

While the Americans on the ground found themselves disorientated and confused, the Germans had no clearer idea of what was happening. Lost Americans did the one thing they could do – cut the enemy's communications. Telegraph poles were blown up and wires cut, and German units found themselves isolated. Even reports that did reach the German command posts were garbled and incomplete. The German commanders could make little sense of the wide dispersal of the American landings and the High Command decided that the attack on the Cotentin Peninsula was a diversion.

On the ground, the American paratroopers outnumbered the German defenders two to one and, with the dawn, they began to make headway. The 506th Regiment, whose target was to capture the dry land to the rear of Utah Beach, managed to assemble two battalions. They seized and held the nearby roadways. Then one battalion routed the German defenders at Pouppeville, while the other fought its way against fierce resistance to the southern end of the beach.

Lieutenant-Colonel Steve Chappius found that the rest of his 502nd Regiment had landed three miles south of the drop zone. Nevertheless, he rounded up a dozen men and struck out for his objective, the powerful artillery battery at St Martin. When he arrived, he found that the guns had been removed. He reported this to General Taylor, who had set up divisional headquarters in an old monastery about a mile away.

One of the paratroopers' main aims was to clear the way for the second wave of the invasion – the glider force. The idea of using gliders also came from the German actions on 10 May 1940, when ten DFS 230 gliders, carrying nine paratroopers each and towed behind Junkers 52 transport planes, landed in a grassy compound on top of Belgium's allegedly impregnable Fort Eben Emael. This cleared the way for the German Panzers to outflank the Maginot Line. The British began training their own glider force after Dunkirk and the US Army Air Force began training glider pilots in May 1942.

The British used the Horsa, a high-winged 67-foot monoplane with an 88-foot wingspan. This could carry thirty men, or a jeep and ten men, and weighed eight tons when loaded. They also deployed the massive Hamilcar glider with a take-off weight of eighteen tons. This could carry forty men and even a light tank, and its 110-foot wingspan dwarfed the Halifax that towed it.

The Americans plumped for the smaller Waco, which carried fifteen men. Prefabricated in Ohio, they were shipped to England where they were to be assembled. Initially untrained British civilians were employed, but of the first sixty-two they put together, fifty-one were not airworthy. The semi-skilled airmen from the US 1st Air Force then stepped in and assembled another two hundred – a hundred of which were destroyed by a thunderstorm. With just five weeks to go before D-Day, glider mechanics were flown in from the US. Working around the clock, they assembled 910 Wacos.

More than a hundred were to land in the Cotentin drop zones, just two hours after the paratroopers. They would carry the essential 57mm anti-tank guns that would be needed if the Germans counter-attacked. But the scattered paratroopers had had no chance to prepare the gliders' landing sites. Many disintegrated on landing. Many fields in the drop zone were too small to land in, resulting in gliders crashing into buildings or hedgerows. These were a lot thicker than expected. Although they could be seen by aerial reconnaissance, they were assumed to be like the hedges in England that could be cleared by foxhunters. Actually, they were six feet high or more and impenetrable. The trees were also taller than expected, making it almost impossible to clear them and land without hitting the hedge at the other end of the field. It was one of the major failures of intelligence. Of the 957 men of the 82nd Airborne's glider force who landed in Normandy that night, twenty-five were killed, 118 wounded and fourteen were missing – giving an overall casualty rate of sixteen per cent before they even got into action. Four of the seventeen anti-tank guns they carried with them were unserviceable, as were nineteen of the 111 jeeps. A second wave of gliders that landed on the evening of 6 June suffered even worse losses and not one of the Wacos that landed in Normandy survived intact.

The British airborne operation away to the east aimed to take control of the five-mile area between the Rivers Orne and Dives to protect the flank of the seaborne landings from the German armoured reserves, massed east of Caen. It was to be undertaken by the 6th Airborne Division, who were to destroy most of the bridges over the Dives to prevent a German counter attack and capture intact the bridges over the Orne and the Caen Canal so that reinforcements could reach them from the beaches. Again one of the major hazards they would face was a flooded area.

The paratroopers were to go in and mark out the landing zones with flares. An hour and forty minutes later the gliders were to arrive. As it was the gliders turned up only about five minutes after the paratroopers had gone in and they had had no time to find the landing zones. When the gliders were cast free by their Halifax tow planes, they descended rapidly; visibility was poor and there were no flares in position on the ground to tell them where to aim for. But one Horsa landed so close to the Caen Canal Bridge – known to pos-

terity by its codename Pegasus Bridge – that it came to rest with its
nose inside the wire defences of the bridge. The lone sentry on the
bridge thought a bomber had crashed. Men jumped out of the
wrecked glider. The first few were cut down by machine-gun fire.
But within three minutes the vital bridge was in British hands. More
gliders landed nearby. One broke in half. Most of the men inside
were injured and one was thrown into the canal and drowned. The
captors of the bridge had lost their radio equipment in the drop and
were unable to contact brigade. But they did make contact with
another glider company who had taken the Orne Bridge.

The 9th Parachute Battalion under Lieutenant-Colonel Terence
Otway was charged with taking the coastal battery at Merville. The
battery's two artillery pieces and ten heavy-machine-guns threatened both the invasion fleet and the British invasion beaches. It
was defended by machine-gun pits, ringed by barbed wire and
minefields and garrisoned by two hundred men. On the night of 5
June, its reinforced concrete fortifications were attacked by a force
of one hundred Lancaster bombers, but they scarcely caused any
damage. Otway was to be dropped a mile-and-a-half away at 0050
and take the battery by 0515. He was then to send up a Very light,
otherwise British warships would start a naval bombardment,
though no one thought it likely that naval guns would succeed when
a hundred Lancasters had failed.

Things began to go wrong when Otway's planes came under
heavy anti-aircraft fire over the coast. A direct hit on the tail of
Otway's own plane made it impossible to steer. Although they were
nowhere near the drop zone, Otway and his men jumped. They landed in an old Norman farmhouse which the Germans were using as a
headquarters. One even crashed through the roof of the conservato-
ry, much to the surprise of the Germans. But some Canadian
paratroopers who had landed nearby opened fire and the Germans
fled. Running well behind schedule, Otway finally reached the
assembly point at 0200. But by 0230 he had only mustered 150 men;

650 were missing. They had lost all their heavy equipment, including their radios; they still had a Very pistol, however. They quickly advanced on the battery at Merville, arriving there with an hour to spare. Fortunately, their reconnaissance party had dropped on target and had already cut the barbed wire and marked a path through the minefield. But as soon as the demolition squad blew up the last of the barbed wire, the German machine-guns opened up. Otway's men were caught out in the open, but some of them made it into the defensive trenches inside the wire, leading up to the walls of the fortifications. They began pouring machine-gun fire through the embrasures, causing a blizzard of ricochets inside, and the Germans quickly surrendered. The Very light went up fifteen minutes before the naval bombardment was to start. Seventy-five British troops – half of Otway's party – had been killed or wounded, while only twenty-two of the two hundred German defenders survived.

But this was the one success of the 9th Parachute Battalion. Mistaking the Orne for the Dives, the pilots dropped the rest of the battalion in the wrong place. Some landed in the American sector. Others were captured or killed in skirmishes, while nearly two hundred men were never found. Otway and his men ran into more trouble later. When they left the Merville area, they were mistaken for a German detachment and were bombed by the USAAF.

One of the Dives bridges was taken out by a single British sergeant who, having borrowed some explosives from some Canadians who were not supposed to be there, walked up to the bridge unchallenged, planted his borrowed explosives and blew it up. The most important bridge over the Dives was at Troarn. This carried the main road from Caen to Le Havre and Rouen. Although the bridge was within striking distance of the British beaches, it was outside the perimeter secured by the paratroopers. A party under Major J.D.A. Rosveare was to land in gliders with jeeps and trailers carrying the demolition charges and make a dash for the bridge before the Germans knew what was happening. The landing, as usual was confused. Major Rosveare mustered just seventy-three of his men, with no jeeps and trailers. They collected all the explosives they could find, loaded them on to handcarts that they found in local farmyards and set off. The first road sign they passed told them they were eleven kilometres from Troarn and they realised that they could not make it there by dawn on foot. At this moment, a Royal Army Medical Corps jeep with a trailer happened by. Rosveare commandeered it, unloaded the medical supplies, loaded what explosives it could carry and sent the rest off with a detachment to blow another bridge nearby. When Rosveare and his party reached the village of Troarn they crashed into a roadblock made of wire. The German sentry loosed off one shot, then ran. But it took valuable minutes to extricate the jeep. The party then careered on though the village, shooting wildly at any German who showed himself. Rosveare lost two men, either to enemy fire from a machine-gun post or they might simply have fallen off the speeding jeep. When they reached the bridge they found it unguarded. It took two minutes for Rosveare and his men to blow it. They abandoned the jeep and disappeared into the undergrowth. By evening they had found their way to British lines, by which time the remaining bridges had been dynamited and the British forces landing on the beach were safe from any armoured counter-attack from the east.

Although the British airborne troops had achieved their objectives more successfully than the Americans, both had managed to spread confusion among the enemy. This did not mean, however, that there was not serious opposition waiting for them in the area. At 0130 Colonel Hans von Luck of the 125th Regiment of the 21st Panzer Division got his first reports of the airborne landings. Immediately, he gave orders for his regiment to assemble and within the hour his officers and men were lined up beside their tanks, which had their engines running. Von Luck's plan was to go and seize Pegasus Bridge from the British, but the only person who could give the order for the Panzers to go into action was Hitler and

Hitler was asleep. So was Von Rundstedt and Rommel was at home with his wife. In St Lô, a birthday party for General Marcks had ended around one o'clock. Marcks was just about to retire for the night when his operations room informed him that there was a great deal of aerial activity over the Cotentin Peninsula. He telephoned General Max Pemsel at the Seventh Army headquarters in Le Man and told him that he believed the airborne landings were not isolated raids. Pemsel woke the Seventh Army's commander, General Friedrich Dollmann, in Rennes and told him that the invasion had begun.

He also woke General Hans Speidal, Rommel's Chief of Staff, with the news. Speidal called Von Rundstedt. Admiral Kranke and Luftwaffe commander Field Marshal Hugo Sperrle also called Von Rundstedt with news of enemy activity. However, between them, they decided that this was not the long-awaited invasion. Just before 0300, Pemsel phoned Speidal again, saying that the air drops were continuing and enemy ships had been seen off the east coast of the Cotentin Peninsula. Speidal was still not convinced and told Pemsel that the parachutists were probably secret agents being dropped to aid the Resistance, or Allied airmen who had bailed out of damaged planes. However, both the German Seventh Army and the 82nd Corps were now on the alert. Their switchboards tried to make contact with forward units, but failed. The phone lines had been cut. The Luftwaffe were scrambled, only to find themselves chasing strips of aluminium foil miles away from the aircraft that were dropping paratroopers and gliders over Normandy. Further confusion was generated when British radio operators cut in on the Luftwaffe frequency and started issuing misleading orders.

6

SWORD BEACH

SWORD WAS THE MOST easterly of the invasion beaches. It ran the two miles from Lion-Sur-Mer to Ouistreham and the mouth of the Orne Canal. It was the key beach in Montgomery's invasion plan, putting the Allies within striking distance of Caen, whose capture – Montgomery hoped on the first day – would prevent any reinforcements coming in from the Pas de Calais. The first on station at Sword was the seven-metre-long midget submarine X23, under the command of Lieutenant George Honour. The X23 had set off from England along with X20, which headed to Juno Beach, at 1800 hours on the night of Friday, 2 June. They had been escorted by trawlers past the Isle of Wight, then they dived and made off for their separate destinations.

Just before dawn on Sunday, 4 June, X23 surfaced to find that it was exactly on station. The Germans had kindly left a light on to mark the mouth of the Orne River. As dawn broke, the midget submarine dived to periscope depth and Lieutenant Honour took bearings from church steeples and other landmarks to check he was in position again. Then they sank to the bottom, dropped anchor and waited. At midday on Sunday, the X23 rose back to periscope level to see lorry loads of German troops coming down to the beach to swim. Plainly they suspected nothing.

At midnight the X23 surfaced to listen for radio messages. They received the coded signal, 'Your aunt is riding a bicycle today.' This meant that the invasion had been delayed for a day due to the weather. The X23 sank to the bottom again and the five-man crew settled down for their long wait. Some tried to sleep in shifts in the two bunks. Others played poker. They were nervous and tetchy because they could not smoke. They also did not know how long they could stay down. Their oxygen supply came from bottles taken from German planes shot down over England and no one knew how long they would last.

The X23 surfaced again twenty-four hours later. This time there was no postponement message and they dived to the bottom again to ready themselves for action. At 0500 they surfaced. The weather was still bad, with the swell running at between one and three metres. With waves breaking over the submarine, they had to erect an eighteen-foot mast with a green light on top of it as a marker for the first wave of the seaborne assault. According to the plan one crewman was to take a rubber dinghy ashore to set up a final marker for the assault on the beach, but the swell was too big to launch the dinghy so that part of the plan had to be abandoned.

The mast was erected successfully by 0520 and a sonar beacon under the submarine was switched on. Soon after, as dawn broke, all hell broke loose. The Eastern Naval Task Force opened up and five-inch shells from its destroyers and fourteen-inch shells from its battleships came screaming overhead. Bombers and fighters were also attacking the beaches and Honour had his cap blown off by the blast of the rockets from fired from an LCT.

Unlike the deserted beaches where the Americans landed, the British beaches had been holiday resorts before the war and were built up. Both the Germans and the Allies had advised the inhabitants to evacuate the area. Many had. But those French civilians who stayed behind suffered terrible casualties.

By 0530 British soldiers were mustered on the boat decks of the landing ships, infantry (LSIs) which were hove to ready to launch the assault. Men from the South Lancashire and East Yorkshire Regiments clambered onto their LCAs and were lowered into the swell. They were to be followed by battalion headquarters and reserve companies. As they headed for the beaches past HMS *Largs*, a bugler of the East Yorkshire sounded a general salute. This was acknowledged by Admiral Talbot and the Divisional Commander, General Tom Rennie.

The first wave of the seaborne invasion was the amphibious tanks which were launched out to sea. Thanks to X23, they were on target. Once they were on their way to the beach, Honour tied a white sheet to the mast of the midget submarine, to ward off collisions with the incoming force, and made his way back to England. The amphibious tanks were to have been launched seven thousand yards from the shore but, due to the heavy seas, the LCTs carrying them took them to within five thousand yards of the beach where they were launched at around 0600. But the wind and the swell meant that the amphibious tanks made slow progress. Some sank in the heavy seas and one disappeared in twenty-five feet of water when it was struck by the bow of its own LCT. Although the amphibious tanks were supposed to have arrived on the beach first, they found themselves passed by LCTs carrying some of Hobart's more specialised Funnies, then the LCAs carrying the first infantry assault groups.

Fortunately, the primary defences of the beach were out of action. The Merville battery had already been taken and destroyed, while the Le Havre battery had spent the morning in an artillery duel with HMS *Warspite*.

While the lead infantry huddled in their LCAs, the artillery in the landing craft behind them opened up as they ran in. At around 0630, 15,000 yards from shore, they adopted an arrowhead formation, attended by a motor launch equipped with radar to calculate the opening range. At 0644 – one minute late – the first ranging rounds of white tracer were fired by A Troop of the 7th Field Regiment. They were joined by gunfire from the battleships, cruisers and destroyers at 0650. And the self-propelled guns of the 3rd Division Artillery opened up at 10,000 yards.

Each of the field guns on the landing craft had a hundred rounds stacked on the deck to be loosed off during the run-in. Most were high explosive, though smoke shells were also used. With Gun Positions Officers announcing the steadily decreasing range over the Tannoy, over two hundred rounds a minute were landing on the foreshore. Some 6,500 had been delivered by the time the bombardment had finished at 0725. Meanwhile the cardboard cylinders the shells were packed in – along with the expended cartridge cases – were thrown overboard, leaving a trail the next wave of landing craft could follow.

The enemy returned fire with 88mm gun batteries a couple of miles inland and mortars and machine-gun fire from pillboxes and defensive positions set up in the remains of the seaside villas along the top of the dunes. The water round the leading landing craft was soon foaming. The artillerymen grew concerned that, in the heavy swell, some of their own shells were falling short so the range was rapidly increased. When the bombardment was over at H-5, the LCTs carrying the field artillery turned away and awaited their appointed landing time which was H+195.

As they approached the beaches, Major C.K. 'Banger' King of the 2nd Battalion, East Yorkshire Regiment, read inspiring extracts from Shakespeare's *Henry V* over the Tannoy, while Brigadier Lord Lovat, commanding officer of the commando brigade, had his piper play a highland reel. The lead LCAs hit the beaches along with LCT carrying Hobart's Funnies at 0726. As the infantry ran down the ramp into the surf, Royal Marine frogmen went over the sides of the landing craft to begin work on submerged beach obstacles.

Next the amphibious tanks arrived after a run-in of almost an hour. As soon as their tracks hit the shelving sand of the beach, they began to rise out of the water. Once the bottom of the flotation shirts were clear of the water, the air was released, the struts holding them in place were broken and the tank was ready for action. Within a minute they were pounding the enemy positions in front of them with shells and machine-gun fire. The enemy replied with 88mm mortars and machine-guns, mainly aimed at the infantry who were still struggling ashore. Smoke gave the infantry some cover, but machine-gun fire running along the length of the beach took its toll.

Captain Kenneth Wright, an intelligence officer with No. 4 Commando, suffered numerous shrapnel wounds before he even hit the beach when a mortar exploded near his landing craft. Nevertheless, he found himself dropped in three feet of water, fifty metres from shore at around 0745. When he reached the beach he found himself among a good many casualties, many of whom had been hit in the water. They were dragging themselves up the beach as the tide was coming in fast. The beach was crowded and the commandos had to queue up to file through the wire at the back of the beach which was the only exit. Wright was attended to by the corps medical officer, who was also wounded. They comforted themselves with calvados and, after twenty-four hours on a stretcher in the open, Wright was shipped back to hospital in England.

Among the infantry, casualties were heavy, but most of the men made it across the beach into the dunes. This left them temporarily helpless as they had outrun their tanks, some of which found themselves stranded, having dropped their flotation shirts, by the incoming tide. Others were hit, immobilised but still firing. The infantry who had made it into the dunes soon took over the task of putting down suppressing fire.

One of the major threats was Strongpoint 0880, codenamed Cod. This was a pillbox surrounded by a zigzag of trenches, which stood almost directly across the beach from where B Company of the East Yorkshires had landed. The company commander Major Harrison was killed almost immediately. Lieutenant Bell-Walker took over and decided that, if he was going to save his men, he had to do something about Strongpoint Cod. With suicidal bravery, he managed to creep around behind it, toss a grenade through the gun slit and follow up with a burst of Sten gun fire. He was cut down by machine-gun fire from the rear positions, but his company got off the beach more or less intact.

When the first wave of LCTs discharged their Hobart's Funnies, the Crabs drove up the beach with their chain-drums flailing to explode mines. At Lion-sur-Mer, a German anti-tank gun was in action, but a bridge-carrying Sherman dropped its bridge directly onto the emplacement putting the gun out of action. Other Hobart's Funnies set various ingenious explosives to blow gaps in the barbed wire and dunes. Bundles of logs were dropped into anti-tank ditches and bridges were laid over the sea walls. These allowed the Crabs, which had made several passes down the waterline and back, to deploy inland to clear the way for the troops.

The immediate area of the beach had been cleared of the enemy as early as 0830. But a strongpoint five-hundred metres inland, that boasted five multi-gunned machine-gun posts, three 81mm mortars, a 75mm and a 37mm gun, and two 50mm anti-tank guns, took three hours to clear and cost the invaders dearly. The German resistance there was only overcome by a joint effort of the East Yorkshires and South Lancashires, along with support tanks and infantry from the 5th Battalion Kings Regiment and elements of No. 4 Commando. The arrival of a machine-gun platoon from the 2nd Battalion Middlesex Regiment with universal carriers finally cleared the German trenches and fifteen survivors surrendered at 1000 hours.

By 0900 elements of the South Lancs had pushed south and taken the village of Hermanville, which was held by two hundred Germans. A Company, which had turned west found itself held up by snipers and machine-gun fire from the German stronghold code-named Trout in Lion-sur-Mer itself. In a nearby wood, the Germans had a battery, protected by trenches and sandbags, that continued to lay down fire across the beach as the Suffolks were coming ashore. A naval forward observer with the commandos only got within range at 1441. He called in a bombardment from the Polish destroyer *Slazak*. After an hour and almost a thousand rounds, the *Slazak* had to break off, but the battery remained in operation for another two days. Despite this German battery, the odd mortar and occasional sniper fire, the fighting on the beach itself was over and men moved at a leisurely pace off the beaches, towards the fighting which was now taking place inland.

Offshore, the Norwegian destroyer *Svenner* had been sunk by a German E-boat and spread of torpedoes narrowly missed HMS *Largs*. Meanwhile on the ship's bridge, there was a heated argument between General Rennie, who wanted to take the Headquarters of the 3rd Infantry Division ashore immediately, and Admiral Talbot, who insisted that he was in charge of the landing and the general would land when he said so. Eventually at 1030 hours, Rennie was allowed to disembark and spent the rest of the day speeding between his units, encouraging them to push forward.

As the initial wave of infantry had been engaging the enemy, the Royal Engineers had been working on the beach obstacles. They had suffered badly under enemy fire and some had drowned. On D-Day, the sappers would suffer 117 casualties and twenty-six Crab flail tanks were knocked out with forty-two casualties among their crew. By 1030, the tide – aided by a strong wind – was covering the sand rapidly and the sappers turned their attention to clearing the exits from the beach. Clearance teams went in to remove mines, stakes and other obstacles at the top of the beach that would slow the landing of further troops. This operation was slowed by the need to remove knocked-out tanks that were scattered along the beach and were blocking the exits. The only way for armour to get clear of the beaches was to move westwards, then down the road to Hermanville which ran along a narrow causeway over the flooded marshland behind the dunes. The delay in clearing the exits caused a back-up. Vehicles choked the narrow strip of sand, which was all that was left of the beach. Fifty self-propelled guns stood in the surf, firing inland. And by 1200 it was decided that landings would have to be suspended for thirty minutes to allow the traffic jam to clear.

Fortunately, by mid-morning the accuracy of the German

shelling of Sword Beach had been drastically reduced because their forward observers had been killed, captured or had fled to the rear. The British soon realised that Germans were then ranging on the barrage balloons that had been flown over the area to discourage air attacks. As the skies belonged to the Allies, these were cut free.

The commandos, which included a large French contingent, spearheaded the fighting inland. Moving with a little more dash and determination that the other infantrymen, they overcame the German defenders in Ouistreham, where there was a monument commemorating the defeat of a British invasion in 1792, and in the casino at Riva-Bella in heavy fighting. One French boy, delighted to be liberated, remarked how thoughtful it was of the British to bring along soldiers who spoke French.

Major R. 'Pat' Porteous lost nearly a quarter of his men by the time they had got over the seawall and casualties would have been worse if their smoke grenades had not impeded the aim of the German machine-guns in the pillbox to their left. Their objective was a coastal battery, but when they reached the battery they found that it housed only telegraph poles. The guns had been moved three kilometres inland a few days before, and they began shelling the old battery position as soon as the British reached it. The bombardment was directed from a fire-control tower in a medieval fortress. Snipers there also harassed them. They tried to storm the tower, but the Germans rolled grenades down on them. A PIAT (Personal Infantry Anti-Tank) hollow-charge missile fired at the tower had no effect and their flame-thrower did not have enough pressure to reach the observers. So Porteous and his men gave up and headed for Pegasus Bridge.

After the shock of the initial attack, the Germans began hitting back. By the time Lord Lovat hit the beaches, they were laying down accurate mortar fire at the water's edge. But that did not stop the legendary Lovat striding up the beach with his piper. Nor did it stop a beautiful eighteen-year-old French girl named Jacqueline Noel tending the wounded. She had come down to the beach to collect her swimming costume and got through the German lines by wearing a Red Cross armband. Once she was on the beach, she could not get back again so did what she could do for the injured men. She later married a British soldier who had landed on D-Day.

Private Harry Nomburg, a central European Jew who was serving under the name Harry Drew in case of capture, fell in at Lovat's side. While wading ashore, he had lost the magazine from his Thompson submachine-gun and hit the beaches without a round. Nevertheless, once he crossed the seawall two German soldiers surrendered to him.

Colonel Peter Masters, a Viennese Jew also in 10 Commando, noted that men dashed ashore. They staggered. His orders had stressed the need to get off the beaches as quickly as possible, but he noticed that the infantrymen who had gone ashore ahead of them seemed reluctant to do this. Some had even started digging in, in the dunes. Carrying a bicycle, he made his way across a ploughed field under a mortar barrage towards his assembly point that was at the edge of a small field a couple of kilometres inland. Under sniper fire from the wood, he had to ford a muddy creek with his bicycle held aloft. As he approached the assembly point, the sniper fire grew more intense, but some British tanks came up and started bombarding the woods.

When Masters reached the assembly point, Lord Lovat was already there, along with two prisoners of war. Lovat asked Masters to interrogate them to find out where the German howitzers were positioned. Masters questioned them in German, but they did not respond. This made some of the commandos quite surly, but Masters examined their papers and discovered that one was a Russian and the other a Pole. He remembered that Poles learnt French in school and found that the Pole was only too eager to answer his questions when he spoke French. Lovat, whose French was better than Masters', took over the interrogation while Masters and his bicycle troop made off for Colleville-sur-Mer, later renamed Colleville-Montgomery, in honour of the general. On the way they saw dead cows in the fields; others had been driven mad by the shelling. When they reached the town, they found that it had been badly damaged in the bombardment. Nevertheless it was plastered with posters announcing the invasion and people stood in the doorways, shouting, 'Vive la France!' and 'Vive les Tommies!'.

The bicycle troop under Captain Robertson headed on to Pegasus Bridge. But at the village of Benouville they were halted by machine-gun fire. Robertson, unwilling to risk the life of any of the other men who had been in North Africa with him, sent Masters down the road into the village so they could see where the firing was coming from. He had only recently been attached to the unit. It was broad daylight and there were not ditches or hedgerows to hide in, and Masters considered his chances of survival were slim. But he remembered a scene from the film *Life of a Bengal Lancer*, where Cary Grant, who is just about to be overwhelmed by Indians, saves the day by crying out, 'You're all under arrest!'

So Masters shouted, in German, 'You're surrounded. Give yourselves up. The war is over for you.'

They did not surrender, but nor did they fire. Masters decided that they must have taken him for a lunatic. Then a German popped up from behind a low parapet. Masters dropped to one knee. The German shot and missed. Masters loosed off one round, then his tommy gun jammed. So he threw himself flat on the ground, thinking his lot was now up. But Robinson had seen enough. With fixed bayonets, his men charged the parapet. The Germans retreated leaving one wounded man and a fifteen-year-old Austrian boy. The rest of the Germans took up positions in a nearby house and continued firing until two British tanks arrived. Two well-aimed tank shells demolished the wall of the house and silenced them. Masters and the bicycle troop then continued on their way to Pegasus Bridge. They joined up with the airborne troops on the eastern side of the

Orne at 1300, achieving their first and most vital objective.

The 3rd Division's thrust inland was spearheaded by the 1st Battalion of the Suffolk Regiment, which was the reserve battalion of 8th Infantry Brigade. The rifle companies had moved off the congested beaches had headed for their assembly area that was some 800 metres inland. Even though the air was full of shells and bullets, they suffered few casualties on the way, but they were hampered by the loss of their forward observer bombardment party, which had been wiped out by a mortar as they left their LCA. This meant that they would not be able to call in artillery support from specific warships as they attacked their objectives inland.

When the Suffolks reached their assembled area, they found no cover. The trees that were shown on aerial reconnaissance photographs were missing. They had probably been cut down to make 'Rommel's asparagus'. A German sniper was hidden in the brushwood left behind, though he soon disappeared. Nevertheless, it was decided to move the assembly point to an orchard two or three hundred metres further inland. There they found some Canadian paratroopers who had been dropped in the wrong place the night before. Throughout the morning they had suffered bombing and shelling by their own side. Even so the Canadians were eager to get at the enemy and joined D Company. News came that their armoured support, in the shape of C Squadron 13/18th Hussars, was now ashore, but there was no sign of the rear battalion HQ. It had been in an LCI, whose landing ramps had been hit and put out of action before it reached the beach. So they had to pull off and transfer to another landing craft. They finally turned up an hour late.

A party was sent on the dangerous mission of making contact with the 6th Airborne Division on the Orne river, then the battalion moved off. Their first objective was Strongpoint Morris, a four-gun 105mm battery housed in a two-metre-thick gun emplacement on the edge of Colleville-Montgomery. On the way, they came across a minefield, conveniently marked with a skull-and-crossbone symbol

and a sign bearing the legend *'Achtung Minen'*. But a quick examination of the field showed that there was a gap in it and the
battalion, with its armour support, made off south-eastwards,
towards the village. This had already been taken by No. 6
Commando, who had cleared the pillboxes at the north end of the
village. They were eager to deal with a multibarrelled mortar that
was then bombarding the beaches and the Suffolks' assembly area.
Some of battalion's tank support went with them, but the mortar
unit quickly withdrew. The Suffolks were amazed to see Lovat
strolling through the village as if he was on a country walk – he had
a stick in his hand as he had given his rifle to a private who had
dropped his on the beach. Then, bagpipes playing, Lovat headed off
towards Pegasus Bridge, while C Company began clearing the village. Over a hundred buildings, stretching more than a kilometre
down the road had to be checked as it was known that the Germans
used the village as a billet for gun crews from the surrounding
strongpoints. However the French were eager to help them and at
1000 hours on D-Day morning, Corporal Ashby of C Company
found himself sharing a bottle of calvados with the Mayor of
Colleville on the first floor of the town hall while they discussed the
disposition of the Germans.

The village was cleared without serious resistance. However,
some Germans had gone into hiding. Two found their way into the
church tower and began sniping from there the next day. By that
time, the area was crawling with British armour. A tank put a 75mm
shell though the tower and the two snipers gave themselves up.

Once C Company had cleared the village, B Company began its
assault on Strongpoint Morris. It was well defended with an anti-
aircraft gun to protect it from airborne attack and six machine-guns
trained on an outer belt of barbed wire nine feet wide and an inner
belt three feet wide. Between them there was a minefield of mixed
anti-personnel and anti-tank mines. No activity could be detected
inside the strongpoint, but Major McCaffrey, commanding B

Company, thought this might be a ruse. An initial bombardment by the support battery brought no response, so McCaffrey decided to blow the outer defences with Bangalore torpedoes – long metal tubes filled with explosive – before calling in a more intensive artillery strike. But just as the torpedoes were being laid, a white flag was raised and sixty-seven Germans came out of the emplacement with their hands up. The prisoners were then paraded along the main street at bayonet point to considerable jubilation.

Although it appeared that Morris had given up without a fight, the Germans there had suffered heavy casualties during air raids on 1 and 2 June. The USAAF had hit them again that morning and they had been bombarded by the 6-inch guns of HMS *Dragon* and the destroyer HMS *Kelvin*. However, when the Suffolks took the position, they found that the guns were intact. The emplacement was cleared of the enemy by 1200, but ten minutes later it came under fire from a German battery further inland. Fortunately, the Allied soldiers now had the two-metre walls of the emplacement to protect them and there were no casualties.

After Morris was taken, B Company moved up to support A Company for its attack on Strongpoint Hillman that lay on the road south to Beuville. As Morris, which lay to the west of Colleville, was being shelled, A Company took an easterly route to Hillman. Unfortunately, the Germans appeared to be firing blind and some of their shells fell to the east of the village. One caused seven casualties in 9 Platoon, knocking it out as a fighting unit.

A hundred metres outside the village, the commanding officer met up with a Canadian paratroop officer who accompanied him into a cornfield where they could observe the strongpoint around 150 metres away. The view was somewhat obscured by corn, which was about eighteen inches high. However, they could see the steel cupola of the fort, which was manned by 150 men of the German 736 Grenadier Regiment. The battalion then deployed for the assault, with C Company sending one platoon forward to the flank and moving another up into an orchard on the outskirts of Colleville, while B Company and a platoon from D Company waited in reserve at the south end of the village.

The battalion's 3-inch mortars and a battery from the 76th Field Regiment then began to zero in on the position. But there were difficulties. Major 'Jock' Waring, battery commander, had trouble communicating with his gun line using the radio. Poor radio communication hampered a lot of the operations on D-Day, partially because the equipment was poor and partially because there was so much radio traffic within such a confined area.

Captain Ryley headed out for a detailed reconnaissance of Hillman at 1130 hours. He found it intact. Although there were some bomb craters close to the wire, the fort itself had not been hit, even though it had been a priority target for the USAAF early that morning. By then they had lost the forward observer bombardment party, so they could not call in an artillery strike from HMS *Dragon*.

Inside the fort, the commanding officer Colonel Krug was ready to fight. He had been informed of the airborne landings at 0140 hours by his divisional commander. Throughout the early hours of the morning, he had heard the tanks of the 21st Panzer Division come under attack as they tried unsuccessfully to retake Pegasus Bridge. At dawn, Hillmore provided an excellent observation point to see the huge armada in the Channel and the British troops making their way slowly inland.

At 1310 hours, a five-minute bombardment began, supported by the battalion's 3-inch mortars and the tanks of C Squadron. A breaching platoon from D Company then crept down a sunken path towards the strongpoint. They crawled through the cornfield to the outer wire, supported by A Company who were deployed to either side. The breaching party pushed their Bangalore torpedoes under the outer wire and blew it. Then a mine-clearance party moved in, clearing a three-foot gap in the minefield which they marked with white tape. Bangalore torpedoes were then pushed under the inner wire, but one of them failed to go off, so the platoon commander went back to get another one, an action that won him the Croix de Guerre.

Although all this activity was taking place within fifty metres of the enemy, the Germans seemed unaware of it, until phosphorous grenades were thrown, ostensibly to hide the breaching party's activities. In fact, they drew attention to it and, when the first assault platoon went in, they attracted a hail of machine-gun fire, killing a section commander. The platoon commander Lieutenant Powell tried to knock the machine-gun in the cupola out with an anti-tank gun. But three shots had no effect. The platoon managed to occupy the trenches, but the Germans withdrew into their concrete bunkers and concentrated machine-gun fire on the attackers.

A runner was sent back with a message saying that the platoon had been held up, but he was killed. A second runner got through and another platoon, under the command of the company commander, came up under the cover of smoke and shellfire. Even so, the German machine-gun fire was so withering that only four men got through. Advancing alone, they managed to take some prisoners. Lieutenant Powell went back for reinforcements. He came back with three men, but found the men he had left behind badly wounded. Captain Ryley was also killed going for help and the best the remaining men could do was drag the wounded back to the sunken lane, where the stretcher bearers picked them up to ferry them back to the Red Cross Post that had now been set up in Colleville. For his actions that day, Lieutenant Powell was awarded the Military Cross, but he was killed before he could receive it.

By this time, the rear battalion HQ had managed to negotiate the congested beach with the battery commander's tank and the CO's personnel carrier. When it turned up at Hillman, it gave the battalion effective radio links to the gun line and the tank squadron for the first time. Tanks were brought up to the wire, but they did no good as their 75mm guns made little impression on the emplacement. Even 17-pounder armour-piercing shot had little effect on the cupola, denting it but failing to penetrate, and covering fire from the tanks did not prevent the machine-guns from taking a terrible toll on the infantry trying to infiltrate through the gap they had made in the defences.

The only way for any progress to be made was to make a gap in the outer defences wide enough to get a vehicle through, so the infantry could come up behind them and engage the enemy at close quarters. A new bombardment was called in, but Hillman responded, knocking out two tanks. Other vehicles disabled by mines were now blocking the Norfolk Regiment which was coming up from behind. Flail tanks were requested to cut a wide vehicle path through the outer defences, but before they had turned up sappers had cleared a sufficiently wide gap through the minefield. By that time, though, the tanks had received urgent orders to take on the 21st Panzer Division which was threatening to counter-attack.

The Norfolks tried to skirt Hillman to take the village of St Aubin d'Arquenay in the mistaken belief that it was still held by the Germans, though it had been cleared by commandos some time before. They headed across the cornfield where they became involved in a disastrous firefight, losing over forty men including a company commander, some to friendly fire.

At 1615 hours, tanks from the Staffordshire Yeomanry turned up. They were ordered through the gap. However the lead tank stopped, refusing to run over the body of a dead British soldier. He was told to 'f***ing well get on with it'. Troops followed the tanks through the gap and fanned out, taking cover in shell holes. Again the tanks' main armament made no impression on the cupola and the German machine-gun still presented an ever-present danger to the infantry. Elements of 8 Platoon were within twenty metres of the cupola when a German came running out with his hands up. He was shot dead. Then Private 'Titch' Hunter rose out of his shell hole and walked determinedly towards the cupola, firing his Bren gun from his hip. The machine-gunners in the cupola did not return fire, but a lone German in the trenches shot at Hunter, grazing his forehead. He disappeared into one of the concrete bunkers. Grenades were tossed down the ventilation shafts and the occupants came out with their hands up. Other concrete emplacements were blown up. By 2000 hours, there was no further resistance. Some fifty prisoners were taken and Hunter was awarded the Distinguished Conduct Medal.

The objective at the western end of Sword Beach was to link up with the Canadians landing on Juno Beach about two miles away. The beaches were separated by a series of reefs that hindered access to the shore. Into this gap, the Germans launched their only serious counter-attack of D-Day. Spearheading it was the 22nd Regiment of the 21st Panzer Division under Colonel Oppeln. At 0900 he had received orders to attack the British airborne troops landing east of the Orne but had made slow progress with Allied fighters strafing his column. At 1200, he was ordered to turn around, go back through Caen and attack the gap between the British and Canadian landing forces. At 1900, the 22nd joined up with the 192nd Panzergrenadier Regiment at the jumping-off point for the attack north of Caen. There Oppeln meet General Marcks, who had arrived from St Lô. Together they studied the situation from the top of a small hill.

'If you don't succeed in throwing the British into the sea we shall have lost the war,' Marcks told Oppeln. The colonel got the impression that victory or defeat depended on his ninety-eight tanks and he agreed to attack immediately.

The 192nd Panzergrenadiers went in first. An elite unit, they were equipped with armoured personnel carriers, trucks and a range of small arms. They pushed for the coast and arrived at the beach at 2000, experiencing almost no opposition. However, their thrust alerted the British and Canadians, who brought up tanks and anti-tank weapons. So when the 22nd Panzers went in they had to run a gauntlet of fire. The lead tank suffered a direct hit and exploded. Inside a couple of minutes, five Panzers had been destroyed. The Royal Canadian Air Force then joined the attack. Oppeln had to call off the advance. The best he could hope for was to hold his position and he dug in. The 192nd Panzergrenadiers were left in the gap, stranded, as, by late afternoon, the rest of the 716th Division was in full retreat.

The King's Shropshire Light Infantry, supported by tanks of the Staffordshire Yeomanry, whose objective had been to take Caen, were diverted into action against the 22nd Panzers. They had been delayed by a howitzer battery near Perier where the Germans had fought doggedly. The position had only been taken when a captured Pole showed Major Wheelock, commanding Z Company, a way through the wire at the back of the battery. By 1600 hours, they had secured Bieville but by 1615 they saw the Panzers coming in from the direction of Caen, which halted their advance.

As night fell, the Norfolks and Suffolks dug in, while the 13th/18th Hussars withdrew to get more ammunition. Enemy artillery opened up, hitting the battalion HQ office truck, causing three casualties. D Company's consolidation area was at the Beauvais farm on the ridge to the south of Hillman. On the way there, they killed two enemy snipers and took out someone who showed themselves at the window of the farm. When they attempted to clear the buildings, forty-six men and two officers surrendered from a slit trench. But it was now night and Major Papillon, the company commander, decided to dig in outside the farm rather than attempt to take it in the dark.

By the end of the first day, the British had put 29,000 men ashore at Sword. They had suffered 630 casualties, but inflicted many more and taken large numbers of prisoners. Even as dusk fell landing craft were queuing up to land more men on the beaches and an enormous force was waiting in the transport area in the Channel, ready to be landed the next day. Sections of the Mulberry Harbours were already on their way from England. However, the British invasion force had not secured its vital, though over-optimistic, objective – taking Caen itself. By the end of the first day they were still five kilometres short of the outskirts. But the Germans showed no signs of exploiting this failure. The 21st Panzer Division had failed to push the British back into the sea and the bulk of German armour was still in the Pas de Calais, awaiting an invasion there.

That night a new wave of 6th Airborne gliders came in. This time the weather conditions allowed less troublesome landings. These were followed by a massive airdrop of equipment. As the sky filled with coloured parachutes, the tired and blooded British troops took great heart from this overwhelming display of air power. They also took comfort from the depressing effect that it must have had on the morale of the Germans.

The Suffolks had settled down the for night at Hillman. At 2230, they began preparing themselves for the next day. An hour later patrols were sent out. It had been a long day. For many it had started at 0330 hours, when they were loaded aboard barely seaworthy craft ready for the assault on the beaches. The battalion's objectives had been taken at a cost of twenty-five wounded and seven dead. C Squadron of the 13th/18th Hussars had one dead and seven wounded. The sapper detachment from 246 Company Royal Engineers had one wounded, while the platoon of the 2nd Middlesex had six wounded and one dead when a mortar hit Colleville. They had captured two hundred of the enemy. A greater prize awaited them the following morning. At 0645 hours, Colonel Krug emerged from his underground HQ with his boots sparkling. The British had been squatting on top of his bunker all night without knowing he was there. He was followed by his batman carrying two suitcases, three officers and seventy men. Krug was relieved of his briefcase which contained maps and other documents. These were sent to battalion HQ and, after the requisite amount of heel-kicking, Krug was passed back to the beaches. The Tommies then took the opportunity to search his quarters and found an extensive cellar of champagne.

Although the Germans' one opportunity to push the British back into the sea had been lost, the British were now dug in, holding a defensive line instead of going after the enemy who was now in full retreat. In Caen, two hundred suspected resistance fighters were summarily executed in the jail. The King's Shropshire Light Infantry had pushed one company forward, but had lost Major Steel, their company commander, and were ordered to withdraw. This gave the Panzergrenadiers of the 21st Panzer Division the opportunity to dig in north of Caen. They began fortifying the ridge from La Londe to Lebisey, commanding the approaches to Caen. To their left, they were reinforced by fresh troops from the 12th SS Panzer Division *Hitlerjugend* (Hitler Youth). These men were young, fit men recruited from the Hitler Youth, a whole different kettle of fish from the old men and foreign conscripts the British had met manning the coastal defences.

On D+1 it was the turn of 2nd Warwickshires to push towards Caen. At first light, they cleared Blainville-sur-Orne, where their commanding officer Colonel 'Jumbo' Herdon met Colonel Nigel Tapp and Brigadier Smith to draw up a plan for a single-battalion attack on the Germans at Lebisey. The starting point was to be the stream which lay midway between Blainville and the wood at Lebisey. This was their first mistake. The starting line was not secure and there were pockets of Germans in the area. Moving forward for reconnaissance, Captain H.C. Illing of A Company found himself fired upon. The start of the operation was delayed for an hour, but B and C Companies, who were out of radio communication, began their advance on time without the benefit of a preparatory artillery bombardment. They ran into the 125th Panzergrenadiers, who slaughtered the lead platoon and killed Colonel Herdon. The attack stalled as the Germans brought up their tanks. However, Brigadier Smith thought that the objective had been taken and ordered the carriers, anti-tank guns and forward observers up the hill towards Lebisey. The Germans were waiting. For the British, it was a disaster.

The vehicles were destroyed. Most of the men were killed or captured. Only a few made it back to the battalion.

Part of the problem was that the Warwicks had no armoured support. The tanks of the Staffordshire Yeomanry had run into an anti-tank ditch dug by the Germans from Beauregard to Lebisey and they were hampered by a number of deep stream beds. The 125th Panzergrenadiers, however, were supported by the tanks of the 22nd Panzer Regiment.

The situation was still unclear when, at 1500 hours, Brigadier Smith sent the 1st Norfolks to capture the east side of the road. They met heavy mortar and shellfire and ran into the 192nd Panzergrenadiers who were well dug in. Although they took heavy casualties, the Norfolks reached the wood where they joined up with what was left of the Warwicks there. But both found themselves pinned down and, at 2200 hours, they were ordered to withdraw under the cover of a concentrated barrage from naval and field artillery. Bren carriers, mortars, guns and an anti-tank platoon where lost and the Warwicks lost a total of 150 men, including ten officers. Even Brigadier Smith was lost, temporarily, in the confusion, and spent the night hiding in a barn. He consoled himself with a bottle of champagne when he made it back to his headquarters in Bieville the next morning.

The King's Own Scottish Borderers were on the other flank. A 1210 hours, they pushed forward into the village of Mathieu and found it unoccupied. They moved on down the Douvres road towards Caen, but at the wood at Le Mesnil they were ordered to dig in. Soon after, they found themselves under attack from shells and mortars. Then they heard armour approaching and decided that their only option was to withdraw. With the piper playing 'Blue Bonnets', the King's Own Scottish Borderers charged through out of the forest, expecting to run into Germans. Instead they found that they were being fired on by a reconnaissance patrol from the East Riding Yeomanry who, in turn, had thought they were German. The

Borderers returned to their positions in the woods with their tails between their legs. At 1700 hours, they were joined by the Royal Ulster Rifles. Then D Company of the RUR, supported by a squadron of the East Riding Yeomanry, moved up to Cambes where they came under fire from the Germans, losing two officers and twenty-nine other ranks. They had inadvertently run into a counter-attack by the 25th SS Panzergrenadier Regiment. Supported by five tanks from 12th SS Panzers, they had taken Cambes. In the fighting three British tanks were disabled. But the Allies still had control of the skies. Fighter-bomber attacks and concentrated artillery fire halted the German advance. They were forced to abandon Cambes and dig in along the road to Caen in defensive positions.

To the rear, the Lincolns had cleared Lion-sur-Mer, then moved up to St Aubin d'Arquenay and the Benouville bridges, which were being defended by Fox Troop of 92nd Light Anti-Aircraft Regiment of the Royal Artillery. These bridges were vital for the British to get off the beaches and over the five days following D-Day, the Luftwaffe mounted eight attacks on them, losing seventeen planes to the British defenders.

Ouistreham was cleared. The South Lancashires also cleared the villages of Cresserons and Plumetot, and moved on to Douvres. This allowed the British from Sword Beach to join up with the Canadians who had landed on Juno, though Douvres radar station remained in German hands until 17 June – D+11. The radar facility itself had been bombed out of action three weeks before D-Day itself, but the station had a secure telephone line to Caen and the Germans hung onto it as a forward observation point.

Although the British failed to take Caen again on D+1, their actions on land, along with the continuing bombardment from the guns of the Royal Navy, seriously disrupted any attempt by the Germans to counter-attack. On 9 June, D+3, a new frontal assault was planned. The Royal Ulster Rifles covered the 1,500 metres of open ground from Anisy to Cambes under withering fire to take

the northern half of the village. In this action all three platoon commanders of A Company were killed. C Company followed up,
supported by five tanks which were destroyed by German artillery,
though they did manage to knock out one Panzer. Within an hour,
Cambes was in British hands, though hours of heavy shell and mortar fire followed. In all the RUR lost 182 men, including ten officers.
They were awarded two Military Medals, three Military Crosses
and a Distinguished Conduct Medal for the action. The King's Own
Scottish Borderers who came up to reinforce the RUR in Cambes,
also lost three men killed and thirteen wounded, along with two
forward observers from the Royal Artillery and three officers from
the 2nd Middlesex.

At the same time, 1st Suffolks moved forward to an assembly
point in Le Mesnil, ready for an assault on the village of Galmanche.
However, on reconnoitring the objective, their commanding officer
was badly wounded and the battalion itself was attacked by the
Luftwaffe who dropped fragmentation bombs.

Both sides dug in and for the next two weeks the situation froze
in these positions. Although Montgomery's initial plan called for the
occupation of Caen, he now used the static position at the eastern
end of the invasion beaches as a pivot for the invasion as a whole. It
pinned down the German forces in Normandy, allowing the
Americans on the westerly beaches to push west, then south, then
east without meeting any serious opposition. Not that the situation
for the British forces that had landed on Sword Beach was without
its consolations. Several times a day they enjoyed 'one minute's
worth of hate' when massive salvos of naval and field artillery fire
were brought down on the enemy. Even so a steady stream of British
casualties were returned from the front as patrols probing the
German positions engaged in savage hand-to-hand fighting.

7

JUNO BEACH

THE CANADIANS LANDED on Juno Beach which lay between the two British beaches, Sword and Gold. It centred on Courseulles-sur-Mer, which was the most heavily defended point in the British sector. And at the extreme left of the beach there were the strongpoints of Langrune and St Aubin. They faced nine medium batteries, comprising mainly 75mm guns, and eleven heavy batteries of 155mm guns. However, only two of the fortified bunkers housing them had been completed. The others stood in roofless bunkers and in open earth-banked gun pits. The guns were sighted along the beaches, which were strewn with obstacles just below the high-tide mark.

However, the German strongpoints were a kilometre apart and the 716th Infantry Division, under General Wilhelm Richter, only had horse-drawn transport to haul their guns and supplies. The men manning the strongpoints were mainly under eighteen or over thirty-five. There were some veterans of the Eastern Front in their mid-twenties, but most of them were badly injured or disabled. The numbers were made up by *Ost* battalion troops from Poland, Russia and Soviet Georgia. As one of General Richter's staff officers pointed out, 'We are asking rather a lot if we expect Russians to fight in France for Germany against the Americans.' But fight they would. They had German NCOs to make sure of that and the barbed wire and minefield around the gun emplacements were there as much to keep the *Ost* troops in as to keep the Canadians out.

Certainly, the German troops were no match for the young, tough, fit and well-trained Canadians, who were highly motivated. Canadians had suffered the bulk of the casualties at Dieppe in 1942. The raid was a national disaster and Juno Beach was the place where the Canadians were going to pay the Germans back, and the odds were in their favour, as they outnumbered the defenders six to one. The first wave would put 2,400 Canadians on the beach to face just 400 German troops.

On the morning of 6 June, some 366 ships assembled in an area just five miles wide by ten miles deep off Juno Beach. At 0530, the slowest LCTs, carrying the amphibious tank squadrons began their run in. An hour later, the heavier support craft, with a destroyer escort, set off. Next came the engineering groups who would knock out the beach obstacles. They were followed by the assault tanks, the flail tanks and other specialised vehicles deigned to cope with the beach defences. Behind them were the first wave of the infantry, with two companies of each battalions. The other two companies followed up in a second wave fifteen minutes later. Behind the infantry spearhead were the LCT carrying rocket launchers. Following them were the self-propelled artillery regiments, who would fire three shells every two hundred yards as they sped towards the beaches.

The Canadians were due to land at 0745 hours, but heavy seas made them ten minutes late and most of the assault troops were seasick. They had been given seasickness pills before they left the landing ships, but they had also been fed a warrior's breakfast which did not sit well on a choppy sea. When they began their run in, the increased speed settled the motion, but now spume sprayed over the landing ramps, soaking the troops and chilling them to the bone.

Some of the LCAs found it hard going. Towed craft broke their lines. It was considered too dangerous to launch the amphibious tanks and the decision was made to beach their LCTs, so they could drive straight onto dry land. But after they passed the 7,000 yard mark, the commanding officer of the 7th Brigade, decided his tanks would swim ashore after all, though the sea conditions meant they landed only just ahead of the infantry.

The infantry were expecting little resistance. In their briefings they had been told that all the pillbox, artillery and machine-guns would be knocked out. On the night before D-Day the RAF did drop 5,268 tons of bombs onto these defences; unfortunately it was woefully inaccurate. At first light, the USAAF took over. But visibility was poor and, for fear of hitting the landing craft as they sped towards the beach, they delayed dropping their bombs, which landed harmlessly in land. Not one of the fortifications on Juno Beach had been hit.

The battleships and cruisers of the Royal Navy started their bombardment at 0600. The destroyers joined in at 0619 and the tanks and 25-pounder field pieces on the LCTs started firing at 0710. After that, wave after wave of rockets went in. But all this firepower threw up so much smoke it was impossible to see the targets, let alone aim at them. According to a soldier from the Royal Winnipeg Rifles, 'the bombardment had failed to kill a single German or to silence one weapon.' It was estimated later that only fourteen per cent of Atlantic-wall bunkers were hit. However, the smoke also made it impossible for the coastal defences to take aim at the invasion fleet.

The bombardment ended at 0730 hours. As the landing was delayed, this gave the Germans plenty of time to man their guns. They did not, however, fire on the landing craft as they rode towards the beaches. The Canadians drew some comfort from the silence of the enemy artillery. Even within 2,000 yards of the shore, they only attracted badly-aimed mortar and small arms fire. It was only later, when they hit the shore, that they realised there had been no firing at them when they were out to sea because the guns were sighted along the beaches.

The demolition teams went in first, setting off the small Teller mines that marked the outer reaches of the obstacles. Nearly a quarter of the landing craft were damaged by explosions, but the troops still managed to struggle ashore. Fortunately many of the obstacles were quickly submerged because of the strong north-westerly wind that piled up water over them. By 0800, the first wave of LCAs were dropping their ramps and the assault teams were making their way ashore on foot, but as soon as they made their way through the obstacles and up on to the beach, the Germans started firing.

There was a high sea wall at the back of Juno Beach, but specialised tanks carried bridges to help the infantry over it. Crab flail tanks dealt with the minefield on the other side. Tanks carrying fascines breached the anti-tank ditches, while bulldozers shifted the barbed wire. Once they were through the coastal defences, the Canadians found themselves in flat open country with few fortifications and very little opposition. However the men on the beaches had to suffer intense flanking fire from fortified pillboxes, until tanks with flame-throwers took them out. At Juno Beach one in eighteen was killed or wounded: there were 1,200 casualties among the 21,400 men landed. However, this figure is misleading as most of the men were landed in the late morning or afternoon, while most of the casualties occurred during the first hour when the casualty rate was more like one in two.

The Regina Rifle Regiment landed at Courseulles where the German defences were the strongest. Allied planners had divided the fishing village into twelve sectors. Each of the six seaward sectors were to be taken by one of the six platoons in the two spearhead companies, while the six inland sectors were to be taken by the six platoons in the second wave.

A Company hit the beach at 0809, directly under the three guns of the harbour strongpoint. The three platoons disembarked from their landing craft and ran for the sea wall. As soon as they left the high-tide line they came under fire by the German artillery and machine-guns. Luckily, B Squadron of the 1st Hussars got ashore ahead of them. Their nineteen amphibious tanks had been launched 2,000 yards out and fourteen had made it to the beaches. They began a deadly duel with the German guns. The 88mm gun at the entrance to the harbour and its 50mm companion were silenced when the Shermans' shells pierced their shields. But the Germans'

75mm gun fired almost its entire ammunition stock of two hundred rounds before a Canadian tank put a shell through its embrasure.

While the armour pounded the strongpoints, the infantry worked their way through the trenches, killing any German who would not surrender. The cost to A Company was heavy. Forty-five men of the Regina Rifles were killed on D-Day, mostly in this action. B Company, away to the east, landed at 0815 practically unopposed and cleared their section with little difficulty.

B Company of the Royal Winnipeg Rifles also ran into difficulties. They were fired on while still at sea. They arrived six minutes ahead of their tanks and many were shot while they were still chest-high in water. When the tanks did turn up, there were only six of them, due to an accident at sea. The infantry's only chance was a charge directly at the enemy and, by the time they got into Courseulles itself, only twenty-six men were left standing.

C Company had no problems. It landed to the west of the strongpoint. Clearing a way though the minefield there, it moved out into open country before capturing the village of Graye-sur-Mer. Along with A and D Company and their tanks, they went on to take the German outpost at Creully, four-and-a-half miles inland, though they left the sanatorium to the west of Graye in the hands of some Russians to be cleared up later.

B Company of the Queen's Own Rifles also found themselves in trouble to the east in Bernière. The wind and tide had carried them two hundred yards east of their planned landing position, dropping them directly under the village's two 50mm guns and seven machine-guns. The amphibious tanks of the Fort Garry Horse had not been launched out to sea and were not there to support them. B Company took sixty-five casualties and they huddled under the beach obstacles. Then Rifleman William Chicoski, Lance-Corporal René Tessier and Lieutenant W.G. Herbert made a dash for the sea wall. It was ten feet high at Bernière and it afforded them enough shelter to work their way along to the strongpoint. There they used Sten guns and grenades to overcome the defenders.

The eastern flank of Juno Beach was taken by the North Shore Regiment. They arrived at 0740, at the same time as their tanks, to find the concrete gun shelter that towered above the beach at St Aubin was still intact. Two tanks were knocked out in the surf by the emplacement's 50mm anti-tank gun. It loosed off seventy-five rounds until it was finally silenced by two high-velocity shells from the Fort Garry's Sherman tanks, a sustained bombardment by a 95mm howitzer of a Royal Marine Centaur and a concrete-smashing charge laid by the Royal Engineers.

Along the entire five-mile stretch of Juno Beach, fighting continued for two hours after the Canadians had first hit the beaches. The Reginas found that the tunnels and trenches that they thought they had cleared when they first landed had been re-occupied by the Germans and the Canadians had to do the hazardous job of trench-clearing all over again. On the other side of the harbour, the Royal Winnipegs were fighting the Germans through the ruins of houses there. In Bernières, the Queen's Own Rifles found themselves under attack when they emerged from the landward side of the village and the North Shore Regiment suffered casualties in the booby-trapped house at the rear of St Aubin.

The situation was little better on the beaches. As the landing craft pulled back from the shore they set off more mines and a quarter of the LCAs were out of action. The leading company of Le Régiment de la Chaudière, reserve battalion to the Queen's Own Rifles and the North Shores, lost all but five of its landing craft. The men swam ashore, but those who made it to the beach had to shelter under the sea wall at Bernières until the Queen's Own Rifles returned to relieve them. And the Canadian Scottish, the reserve battalion of the Reginas and the Winnipegs, found itself held up on the beach by a minefield – 14,000 mines had been laid between Bernières and Courseulles – and badly mortared.

Nevertheless at H+2, the two leading brigades were ashore and the reserve brigade, the 1st, and its armoured regiment, the Sherbrooke Fusiliers, were landing against little resistance. The beach was jammed with men and vehicles, while Crabs made gaps through the minefields so they could leave the beach. At Bernières there was an additional difficulty as the area behind the dunes was flooded. An ingenious solution was found. At 1200 hours, a tank was sunk in the mire and used as a pier for a bridge. This bridge remained in place until 1976. When it was replaced, the tank was removed: it is now a local war memorial.

Fighting continued in St Aubin until 1800 and the North Shore Regiment were still engaging the coastal command post of the 2nd Battalion of the 736th Grenadier Regiment at 2000. But otherwise the Canadians pushed on into the countryside with negligible resistance, as the area behind the beaches was practically deserted, both by the French inhabitants and the defending forces. Richter was so short of men that he had no choice but to put them all on the coast itself, and once they were overcome, resistance was at an end. There were a few snipers at Banville and Colombiers-sur-Selles and a little resistance in the village of Anguerny. But even this was overcome by the late afternoon. By the end of D-Day the North Nova Scotia Highlanders, who had landed on the beaches at noon, were at Villon-les-Buissons, just three miles from the outskirts of Caen.

Montgomery and Eisenhower were delighted. The Canadians were deeper into France than any other troops that first day. Better, they had not suffered a tragedy comparable with Dieppe, which had been the great fear. Heavy casualties had been expected. Losses of 2,000, including 600 drowned had been anticipated. In fact, the Canadians suffered just 1,000 casualties, including 335 dead. The Reginas had lost forty-two, the Winnipegs fifty-five and the Queen's Own Rifles sixty-one. These came mostly from the assault groups that had been landed under the strongpoints.

The enemy had been completely overcome. Of the four German

and two Russian battalions stationed in the area, only one battalion at 80 per cent strength could be mustered by the end of the day. To all intents and purposes, the German 716th Division was no more. The Canadians were still a few kilometres short of their D-Day objective: N13, the main road that joined Cherbourg and Caen to Paris. But then, it is generally agreed that all D-Day objectives were wildly over-optimistic.

On 7 June, D+1, the North Nova Scotias, supported by the Sherbrookes cleared the village of Buron and moved cautiously on to St Contest, where they came under fire. A reconnaissance patrol reached the Caen-Bayeux road but heavy shelling forced the battalion to dig in around the villages of Buron and Authie. At about 1300, the Canadians saw Panzers to the east of Authie. The Sherbrookes engaged them and lost two tanks. The North Nova Scotias then found themselves under attack from two waves of German infantry. They were forced to withdraw and fall back to positions south of Les Buissons, where they found that there were only five men left from C Company and a handful from A Company. Late in the afternoon the Sherbrookes counter-attacked at Buron to evacuate the North Nova Scotias pinned down there. They withdrew to Les Buissons where they dug in with the Highland Light Infantry and the Stormont, Dundas and Glengarry Highlanders, while the Panzer attack was halted by a naval bombardment that reduced the villages of Buron and St Contest to rubble within a few minutes. The day had cost the North Nova Scotias over 200 casualties. The Sherbrookes had lost sixty men and more than a third of their fifty tanks.

7th Brigade to the right had reached the Caen-Bayeux road on D+1 and dug in. Late in the afternoon the 3rd Battalion of the 26th SS Panzergrenadier Regiment, followed an hour later by the 2nd Battalion, headed straight for the Winnipeg Rifles who held the railway track to the south of Putot-en-Bessin. Early the next morning, they hit the Winnipegs hard. Only D Company held its ground and the Winnipegs lost the equivalent of two rifle companies.

A costly counter-attack by the Canadian Scottish forced the Germans out of Putot. Instead they turned on the Reginas a few kilometres to the east. Panthers from the 12th SS Panzers drove into the centre of Bretteville, which the Reginas were holding. But by then darkness was falling. This gave the Canadians a considerable advantage as they could get up close with anti-tank weapons. One Panther tank that was attacking battalion headquarters was hit twice by anti-tank shells, then a string of anti-tank grenades blew a track off. The crew got out, but were cut down as they fled. In all twenty-two German tanks went into action in Bretteville during the night, but six were destroyed. This blunted the German counter-attack. However, the Canadians' advance had stalled short of Carpiquet, the airfield for Caen.

On 8 June Montgomery was ashore and he set up his headquarters in the chateau in Creully in the Canadian sector. From there he planned a new strategy to take Caen. On the morning of 11 June, the Queen's Own Rifles and the 1st Hussars were ordered to advance seven miles on the British left flank and take the high ground near the village of Cheux, a few kilometres south of Putot-en-Bessin, believing that the Germans were on the run. Just outside the village of Le Mesnil-Patry they ran into the Germans who called in artillery support and took out six Canadian tanks inside a minute. They had been listening in on the Hussars' frequencies and knew they were coming. The 1st Hussars lost eighty men and thirty-seven tanks, and D Company of the Queen's Own Rifles lost most of the 135 men who had started out. This action resulted in another stalemate and the Canadians remained in an arc north-west of Caen for a month. Both sides dug in and the Normandy countryside was lined with trenches and barbed wire reminiscent of the First World War, with continuous artillery and mortar exchanges taking their daily toll. Even so, the Allies now had a firm hold on the north-west coast of Europe. On D+6 Churchill, Alan Brooke and South African

Prime Minister Jan Smuts all landed on Juno Beach at Graye-sur-Mer and on D+10 King George VI arrived there too.

8

GOLD BEACH

CASTING OFF AT 0615, six miles out from shore, the Royal Engineers and the Underwater Demolition Teams hit Gold Beach at 0753. H-Hour on Gold was one hour later than on the American beaches, as the tide swept from west to east and low tide came later on the British beaches. However, the strong wind was piling up the water so that some of the beach obstacles were underwater before the Underwater Demolition Teams could destroy them.

There were two German concentrations along Gold Beach, one at La Rivière on the left flank where Gold met Juno Beach and one at Le Hamel in the centre. They were in the resort houses that were dotted along the coast, rather than in the concrete emplacements. That meant they could be set on fire by the air strikes and naval bombardment that preceded the landings. Apart from some flak the air strikes on Gold were practically unopposed and the only response to the naval bombardment was some inaccurate shooting by 6- and 8-inch guns in a coastal battery some three-quarters of a mile inland. The British naval guns, by contrast, ranged from five to fourteen inches.

However, there were a series of well-concealed gun emplacements on the steep cliffs near Longues-sur-Mer to the west of Gold Beach which were left unscathed by air strikes and the initial bombardment. Soon after dawn, they began firing on the battleship USS *Arkansas* off Omaha Beach and forced HMS *Bulolo*, the headquarters ship for Gold Beach, to change position. The light cruiser HMS *Ajax*, which had famously seen action off Montevideo against the *Graf Spee* in the Battle of the River Plate, moved in to take on the fortification. Fortunately, the exact co-ordinates of the emplacements had been paced off by the farmer who owned the land and his blind son. They had got the figures to André Heintz, professor of history at Caen University, who transmitted them to England on a home-made radio. The first twenty minutes of the *Ajax*'s bombardment forced the Germans to abandon two of the emplacements because of the concussion caused by the shock of the *Ajax*'s 6-inch shells hitting the concrete. Then a shell entered the embrasure of a third emplacement while a shell was being loaded into the 155mm-gun's breech. The shell went off, setting off the magazine. No-one survived.

Sherman tanks on the LCTs had 25-pounder guns, and more 25-pounder field pieces towed behind them fired three rounds a minute, starting when they were twelve kilometres from shore and ending when they were three kilometres from the beaches. This bombardment and the rockets being fired at the beaches meant the noise on board the LCAs was deafening.

The lead LCAs each fired twenty-four Spigot bombs, containing thirty pounds of high explosive each, from a range of about 400 yards. These were aimed to land among the beach obstacles and clear a path twelve yards wide and eight yards long. The idea was that the amphibious tanks and Hobart's Funnies on their LCTs behind would have a clear lane to the top of the beach, so they could deal with the defenders there before the first infantrymen arrived. The lead LCAs were conscious of the strange silence that engulfed the shore once the naval bombardment was over. They had also been issued with 'sticky bombs', explosive charges that they were suppose to lean over the side and attach to remaining beach obstacles. They were new items of equipment and no one had been trained to use them. Few stuck and those trying to attach them came under sniper fire.

They had major trouble avoiding being run down on the high seas by the LCTs behind who passed them on the run-in. German snipers also prevented the Underwater Demolition Teams clearing lanes of mines. This being the case, the pilots of the landing craft behind them had been told that the best tactic was to approach the shore at full tilt. Twenty of the LCTs hit mines, losing both men and tanks. But two companies of Hobart's Funnies were landed near Asnelles.

When the LCAs bringing the infantry assault teams hit, the men rushed ashore. One commando said that their eagerness to get ashore was because they would rather have fought the whole German army than go back onto the landing ships. Everyone had been seasick after a breakfast of fried eggs washed down with a tot of rum, which was mandatory for all those going ashore. Fortunately, there was little resistance. The enemy strongpoints had been knocked out by the naval bombardment. There was some inaccurate shelling and mortaring from inland, but the German 88 mortar teams on a ridge above the beach were soon silenced by the British 25-pounders. And the defenders on the beaches – largely Russians – were eager to surrender.

However, at Le Hamel a machine-gun team poured fire from a pillbox to considerable effect. More Germans, protected by the remains of the houses and hotels in Le Hamel, maintained withering fire on the beach, which was shrinking rapidly as the tide came in. They were supported by mortar teams to the rear that rained down fire on the invasion force. Further landings there were halted, with the second wave being diverted either side of the strongpoint, which held out until mid-afternoon. Elsewhere opposition was easily overcome. Even the strongpoint at La Rivière only held out until 1000 hours, though it cost the lives of ninety-four men of 69th Brigade, including six officers, to take it. The 47th Royal Marine Commandos landing to the far right near St Côme de Fresne came under heavy machine-gun fire from the German 352nd Division as they tried to negotiate the beach obstacles. This damaged fifteen out of their sixteen landing craft at the loss of forty-three men and their signalling equipment. They headed west towards the small harbour town of Port-en-Bessin where they were supposed to meet up with the Americans from Omaha Beach. The Royal Marines took it from the rear on D+2 at the cost of two hundred lives.

As the lead assault companies of 6th Battalion of the Green Howards landed on the King section of Gold Beach, they saw what looked like a pillbox. Company Sergeant Major Stan Hollis of D Company, a hardened veteran, grabbed a machine-gun, balanced it on the ramp of the LCA and gave the pillbox a burst. There was no response – probably because it was not a pillbox at all but a shelter for the tramline that ran along the sea front. As they hit the beach, Hollis picked up the gun to take it with him, only to burn his hand on the barrel. His colleague Sergeant Hill, who had survived the campaign in North Africa and Sicily, tripped when he left the landing craft and was killed under it as the landing craft drove into the beach. With three mortar men and three machine-gunners, Hollis made it up the high-tide mark. They laid down smoke to cover the rest of the men as they breached the minefield there. This was hardly necessary as the naval bombardment had already filled the air with dust and smoke.

As Lieutenant-Colonel Robin Hastings, the commanding officer of the 6th Green Howards, hit the beach, he saw that A Company was pinned down by a German 105mm gun emplacement and a pillbox. But a tank from B Squadron of the 4th/7th Royal Dragoon Guards, who were supporting 6th Green Howards, managed to 'post' a shell through the emplacement's embrasure, silencing the 105mm. Then Lance-Corporal Joyce, who Hastings had got out of a Glasgow cell after a drunken spree on embarkation leave in Scotland, jumped up on to the sea wall, threw a grenade into the pillbox, then rounded up the survivors. This earned him the Military Medal.

Once Hollis and D Company were through the minefield they headed for their next objective, the gun battery at Mont Fleury. A short way up the road, they came under fire in the area of a house, but they continued towards the battery. Following with company headquarters, Major Ronnie Lofthouse spotted that the small-arms fire was coming from a concealed pillbox and pointed it out to CSM Hollis. Single-handedly Hollis charged the pillbox, Sten gun blazing. The Germans returned fire but miraculously missed. When he reached the pillbox, Hollis shoved the muzzle of his Sten gun through the firing slit and gave it a burst. Lying on the roof of the pillbox, he dropped a grenade through the slit. Once it went off, he jumped down the back and opened the door. He found two dead Germans inside, along with a number of wounded. The rest surrendered. Quickly changing the magazine on his Sten gun, he followed a trench which led to another pillbox, whose occupants surrendered. In all, he had twenty-five to thirty prisoners on his hands. He directed them towards the beach. From there, they would be shipped back to prisoner of war camps in England.

D Company could then move on to the Mont Fleury Battery without risking German fire from their rear. They found that the garrison there had already fled following the air and naval bombardment. C Company, supported by B Squadron of 4th/7th Dragoon Guards, had captured the German position on the Meuvaines Ridge. It had been feared that this was a rocket site. In fact it was a command headquarters. B Company ran into an unexpected minefield, which delayed them. They had also taken a number of prisoners which, like the others, had been sent back to the beaches. Although 6th Green Howards were rapidly ticking off their objectives, their progress was not without cost. The Green Howards were a regiment that were led from the front and a high proportion of their senior officers had been killed or wounded. Nevertheless, they pressed on towards Crépon with Companies B and C leading, D following and A in reserve. As they neared the village, they came under concerted fire. Even though the road through Crépon would be their supply line as they moved south, Colonel Hastings did not want to waste time clearing it. He sent Companies

B and C around the village, leaving D Company to take it.

As the company commander Lieutenant Kirkpatrick had been killed, CSM Hollis took command. He quickly secured the village, but on the Bayeux road he spotted a farm and went to investigate. Inside he found only a small boy, but as he investigated an alleyway that led out to an orchard, a bullet hit the wall just inches from his head. He pulled back, then advanced again on his belly. In the orchard he saw two dogs near a gap in the hedge. They were wagging their tails. To a veteran like Hollis, this meant that someone who liked dogs was hiding in the gap and, as he concentrated on that area, he saw the outline of a field gun.

Hollis reported back to Major Lofthouse, who told him to take a PIAT anti-tank gun and a small party of men and take out the gun. In the orchard, Hollis saw a rhubarb patch. His plan was to crawl along it with the PIAT – a notoriously inaccurate weapon – to get closer to the field gun to take his shot. He would be accompanied by two Bren gunners, the rest of his men ready to give covering fire. Unfortunately, as soon as they showed themselves, they were cut down. Hollis fired at the field gun, but the round fell short. The field gun then traversed towards his position and loosed off a shot. It hit the farmhouse, but Hollis decided that next time he might not be so lucky. He shouted to his Bren gunners to withdraw, then he crawled back up the rhubarb patch, dodged through the alleyway into the farmyard and made his way back to report to Major Lofthouse.

Lofthouse decided that the field gun presented no major threat and could be dealt with later. But then they heard a firefight going on near the farmhouse. It was Hollis's Bren gunners. Exchanging the PIAT for a Bren gun, Hollis went back to get them. He rushed into the orchard, firing from the hip and screaming for the men to get out. They withdrew and, along with Hollis who was miraculously unscathed. the three men rejoined their company in one piece. For this action, and his attack on the pillbox, CSM Hollis won the Victoria Cross. He was the only man to be awarded Britain's highest award for valour on D-Day. That night 6th Green Howards were a mile short of their D-Day objective, St Léger on the Bayeux-Caen road. They had suffered ninety casualties.

Six miles inland from the coast to the right of the beach was a battle group stationed at Bayeux, on which the Germans were depending for their response to an invasion in that area. However, they had set off at 0400 to Isigny, where enemy paratroop landings had been reported. This was something of a wild-goose chase and they were ordered back to their base at 0800. They were to counter-attack towards Crèpon, but the order took an hour to reach them, then it took them five hours to get back, as many of the French trucks they commandeered had broken down. By that time, one battalion had been hived off to face the Americans landing on Omaha Beach. When they reached their assembly point at Brazenville they found it was already in British hands.

About midday, British troops reached the small village of Creully, about five miles inland. The eight men in German uniforms who were to have defended the beach there – five Russians and three Lithuanians – surrendered immediately. The British then pushed on to the N13 which they reached at the village of St Léger, halfway between Bayeux and Caen, at 1500. The squad that arrived there climbed a tree to spy out the land, only to see a German half-track rumble into the village and park at the bottom of the tree while the six-man German crew got out to relieve themselves. Two more German half-tracks arrived. Two of the half-tracks made off – one to the east, one to the west – leaving the third parked in the village square. As soon as the coast was clear the Tommies shinned down the tree, hot-wired the half-track and made off back to Creully where, by then, the British had met up with the Canadians from Juno Beach.

In the afternoon of D-Day, Creully had been the site of a crucial tank action between the 4th/7th Dragoon Guards and German Panzers. Part of 8th Armoured Brigade, 4th/7th Dragoon Guards had been put under the command of 69th Infantry for the invasion with one tank squadron assigned to each infantry battalion. B Squadron would support 6th Green Howards; C Squadron would support 5th East Yorkshires to their left. The plan had been for the tanks to swim ashore, landing five minutes ahead of the assault battalion. A Squadron would support 7th Green Howards, the reserve infantry battalion, and land at H+45. Their tanks had been fitted with flotation screens and a Duplex-Drive that operated a small propeller from the tank's main engine. However, some of A Squadron's Shermans had had their 75mm guns replaced by 17-pounders, which were more effective at knocking out Panzers. As the barrel of the 17-pounder was too long to fit inside the flotation screen, A Squadron's landing craft would deliver them directly to the beaches. At the last minute, they were supplied with a roll of beach matting. When the ramp dropped, two men were supposed to run forward, unrolling this. Then the tank would drive up it. A Squadron were not impressed, having practised the landing without this new-fangled device. During the Channel crossing, the matting disappeared overboard.

As it was, the sea was too rough off Gold Beach to launch the amphibious tanks, so B and C Squadrons were unloaded in shallow water a few hundred yards off shore. They made it to the beach with few casualties. A Squadron who followed up at 0830 lost two tanks which sank in underwater shell holes. After breaching a minefield, they headed down the road past Crépon to Creully with the 7th Green Howards. The 1st and 3rd Troops led, with the 2nd and 4th following with the infantry riding on them. By this time there was little opposition and the few Germans they encountered were eager to surrender.

Their aim was to reach the bridge at Creully as quickly as possible. It was a key crossing point of the River Seulles which otherwise might prove a significant tank obstacle. There were reports that a German Panther tank was holding the bridge, but it had withdrawn before A Squadron arrived. The British tanks quickly crossed the bridge and drove nervously into the village itself. Tanks are more vulnerable in a built-up area where men with anti-tank weapons can get up close in the narrow streets and snipers can pick off the tanks' commanders, who have their heads out of the tank turrets. But A Squadron made it through the village without incident and out into the cornfields on the other side. This was perfect tank country and the experienced tank commander Major Jackie d'Avigdor-Goldsmid deployed his squadron for a rapid push south. Suddenly two of his tanks exploded and he ordered the rest of the squadron to make a dash for a line of trees four hundred yards ahead. They made it, but another tank was hit there. Like the others it burst into flames. The Germans called Shermans 'Tommy cookers' because of their tendency to catch fire when hit. Even though he saw this inferno, Lieutenant Alastair Morrison, leader of the 4th Troop in the rear, made a dash for the trees. When he reached them, he saw another tank go up but, by chance, he spotted a distance gun flash near the bottom of a telegraph pole. He did not dare roll his tank forward to the edge of the trees to engage the enemy directly. Instead, he called in indirect fire, which hit the target with the second shell. Suddenly shells were bursting all around them. Both A Squadron and 7th Green Howards suffered heavy casualties. It was discovered later that the fire came from HMS *Orion* after someone ashore called in artillery support. When they withdrew to a more secure position to tend to their casualties, they were attacked by an American Thunderbolt fighter. It was only on his third pass that he spotted the orange smoke from a smoke grenade Morrison flung into the cornfield to warn the pilot he was attacking friendly forces.

By the end of the day, A Squadron had lost seven killed, four injured and four tanks. But, in all, the British had put 25,000 men on Gold Beach, at the cost of 413 casualties. And the next day they were in a position to take the all-important N13.

When the Germans began their counter-attack on 8 June, elements of General Fritz Bayerlein's Panzer *Lehr* Division were moved up from Chartres to Tilly-sur-Seulles, directly in front of the British positions. The following morning they tried to move around to the left and take Bayeux. The 2nd Battalion of the Panzer Lehr Division had reached the village of Ellon, just three miles south of the town. Despite heavy naval and artillery gunfire, they were confident that they could take Bayeux when they were ordered back to Tilly. The British were now well south of N13. The 1st Dorsets of 231 Brigade had captured the village of Audrieu and the tanks of 8th Armoured Brigade were pushing south to St Pierre and threatening to cut the road that connected Tilly to the 12th SS Panzer Division to the west of Caen.

But confusion reigned. That same morning. General Geyr von Schweppenberg turned up at the headquarters of the 12th SS Division and ordered a new attack, designed to push the British and Canadians into the sea. To the east the 21st Panzer Division was to push north up the River Orne and the Caen Canal. The 12th SS Panzer Division were to push up the Caen-Bayeux road to take on the Canadians, while the Panzer Lehr Division would about face again and take Bayeux. But this time they faced the 7th Armoured Division which had just arrived from Gold. Its orders were to take Tilly and press on to Villers-Bocage. From there, the British forces were to move south-east to Falaise, outflanking Caen. This would give the Allies enough space to station its planes on French soil and maintain its all-important air superiority. The landscape to the south was also far better for the deployment of tanks. This strategy disrupted von Schweppenberg's plan and resulted in confused fighting across the region. Casualties were high, but the British and Canadian progress was relentless. Allied air superiority allowed them to bomb von Schweppenberg's headquarters on 11 June, killing many of his staff and wounding von Schweppenberg himself. And on 12 June General Marcks was killed in an air attack. This left the German forces in Normandy without an effective command structure for two weeks, while the invaders fought ferociously from hedgerow to hedgerow.

Some of the worst of the fighting took place around the village of Cristot on D+5 – 11 June. At the centre of the action, once again, would be 6th Green Howards. Colonel Hastings was summoned to brigade headquarters and told to have his battalion ready to move at 1400. He learnt that 8th Durham Light Infantry, with the support of 8th Armoured Division, had entered Tilly-sur-Seulles, but had been pushed out again by a German counter-attack. A second attack was being planned. The Green Howards were to occupy a small hill just south of Cristot to protect the flank. The task seemed simple enough, but the situation did not fill Hastings with confidence. The planning seemed hurried. There was no time for him to carry out any reconnaissance, though an earlier reconnaissance party had made it nearly to the top of the hill encountering only light opposition. The weather that day was bad. Rain was coming down in sheets, and the countryside around Cristot was the worst kind of bocage country, with small, irregular fields and lots of thick, high hedges concealing paths and roads that were often sunk between high banks. This terrain favoured the defenders. Those attacking would have to take high casualties to take any objective that the enemy was determined to hold on to. Tanks were particularly vulnerable as men with hand-held anti-tank guns could easily lie in wait for them behind the hedges.

Hastings decided to make a sunken track that ran up to the summit of the hill the centre line for the attack. His headquarters would move up it with his two leading companies – B to the right, C to the left – just ahead. They would be accompanied by the tanks of B Squadron 4th/7th Dragoon Guards. A and B Companies would follow, supported by C Squadron, while A Squadron would wait behind to bring up the battalions anti-tank guns and mortars once the objective had been taken.

Things began well enough. B and C Companies crossed the

Cristot-Tilly road to the south of the village without incident. Then C Company came under heavy fire from a farmhouse around a hundred yards ahead. The company commander, Captain Chambers, who had already been wounded on D-Day, was killed. The tanks of B Squadron were hit and the casualties began to mount. Soon the left came to a halt.

Then it was B Company's turn. Heavy fire to the right brought the advance to a halt altogether. An attempt to outflank the Germans failed and Major Young was wounded. Private Leary won the Military Medal for dragging Young from the battlefield and saving his life, despite being wounded himself. B Company's second-in-command Captain Mitchell had also been killed, so Hastings moved A Company up behind B Company and tried a flanking movement to the right again.

The battalion headquarters then came under fire. Hastings withdrew and sent D Company up the track to clear it. Major Lofthouse sent a tank up the track itself, with 17 and 18 Platoon on the right and 16 Platoon, headed by CSM Hollis, on the left. Although the high banks on either side of the track protected them from flanking fire, they found themselves under fire that was coming directly down the track. As 17 Platoon took casualties, Hollis crawled forward. He saw two Germans loosing off regular bursts of fire, then popping their heads up at regular intervals to see what effect they had had. Hollis found that he had no grenades in his pouches, but borrowed one from one of his company. After the next burst of fire, he flung it at the Germans. It was only when it had left his hand that he realised he had forgotten to pull the pin. But the enemy did not know that. Lofthouse, hoping that they would keep their heads down waiting for it to go off, charged up the track and finished the crouching Germans off with his Sten gun.

Hastings stopped at the point where Hollis had despatched the two Germans to take stock of the situation. C Company had taken the farmhouse and A and B Companies had nearly reached the top of the field. But bodies were strewn around the battlefield. They had lost a number of tanks and valuable manpower was having to be employed herding together the Germans they had captured. Despite the Germans' dogged defence of the position, Hastings decided to push on. Soon after, A Company commander Major Honeyman was killed, when he attempt to extricate Company Sergeant Major Calvert and his platoon from an exposed forward position. Later Calvert returned safely with his men and was award the Distinguished Conduct Medal. Major Honeyman was awarded a Military Medal posthumously for his leadership of A Company on Gold Beach on D-Day.

With the tanks unable to move forward, the advance stalled once more. Considering the situation, Hastings decided that the battalion neither had the officers or the NCOs to continue the attack and he ordered them to dig in. If they could hold their ground, brigade could send up another battalion to move through their position. But as the evening wore on, no fresh men turned up and Hastings feared that the Germans were preparing a counter-attack. With nightfall approaching, he knew that the tanks would have to pull back to safe areas for routine maintenance. Brigade gave him permission to withdraw and the 4th/7th Dragoon Guards carried out the wounded. The Green Howards had taken 250 casualties and gained nothing. It was clear that the Germans had recovered from the initial shock of the Allied invasion and were now fighting back. In fact, 8th Armoured Brigade's push on Tilly was forestalled by an attack by the 2nd Battalion of Panzer Lehr up the road to Audrieu. The Germans had also been trying to hold the hill south of Cristot to protect the flank of their armour. Fourth Panzer broke through the British lines, but they were quickly destroyed. The rest of the attack was repulsed. But they held on to the hill, which overlooks Carpiquet airfield and the westerly outskirts of Caen it was only relinquished on D+19, 25 June.

It was not just the 6th Green Howards and 8th Armoured

Division that were stalled along a line that ran though Cristot. On 10 June, 7th Armoured Division had passed through the 50th Division on the Bayeux-Tilly road. At dusk, they bumped into the Panzer Lehr Division, who were under orders to advance on Bayeux at Bucéels two miles north of Tilly. The following day the situation remained stalemated. On the morning of 12 June, General Erskine of 7th Armoured Division and General Bucknal of XXX Corps met to discuss what to do. They had intelligence that there was a gap between the Panzer Lehr Division, which was in the Tilly-Lingèvres area, and Caumont, which was then being besieged by the Americans. If 7th Armoured Division could mount a quick attack down the road that ran through St-Paul-du-Vernay, Briquessard and Villers-Bocage they could seize the high ground to the rear of the Panzer Lehr Division and cut them off.

The thrust was headed by 22nd Armoured Brigade reinforced by a lorried infantry battalion, the 1st/7th Battalion of the Queen's Regiment. Everything went well until they met opposition in the area of Livry at 1600. By 2000, this had been cleared by the 1st Battalion of the Rifle Brigade, the motor battalion with 22nd Armoured Brigade. But still six miles from Villers-Bocage, Brigadier Robert 'Looney' Hinde decided to stop for the night so that maintenance work could be carried out on the tanks. The stragglers could then catch up and he hoped that contact could be made with the Americans to their right. At 0530 the next morning they pressed on to Villers-Bocage. Outside the town, they were told by French citizens that it was clear of Germans. They took the town and the tanks of A Squadron, 4th County of London Yeomanry, the Sharpshooters, with A Company of 1st Rifle Brigade. Lieutenant Colonel Lord Cranley, the Sharpshooters' commanding officer, went on through the town and up the road to Caen on take the high point there. They had reached their objective and were making tea when everything came unstuck.

On D-Day, 101st SS Heavy Tank Battalion had been stationed at

Beauvais, north-west of Paris. Hastily posted to Normandy, they arrived in the Villers-Bocage area on 12 June. Due to regular attacks by the Allied air forces, 2 Company now consisted of just five Tiger tanks. But they were commanded by the legendary Lieutenant Michael Wittman, an ace who had knocked out 138 enemy tanks. While the rest of his company were performing much needed maintenance in a small wood near the village of Montrocq, around a mile north-east of Villers-Bocage, Wittmann went out on a reconnaissance mission. He was just south of the Villers-Caen road when he was stopped by a sergeant who told him that he had heard the unmistakable sounds of tanks coming out of Villers-Bocage, even though there were no German tanks in the area. Wittmann dismounted and crawled through the hedge that flanked the road. He saw A Squadron and the infantry half-tracks making their way up the hill. The British Cromwell tanks, with their 75mm guns, were no match for the Tiger and its 88mm cannon.

At 0830, Wittman emerged in his Tiger down the track from Montbrocq right into the middle of the British column advancing up the hills. The lead tanks turned their guns and depressed them to fire on the Tiger, but the movement of their turrets was too slow. Two shots from the Tiger knocked out two tanks, blocking the road and making it impossible for other Cromwells to come to the defence of the column. Wittmann then turned his tank down towards Villers-Bocage knocking out the infantry's half-tracks one by one as he worked his way down the line. A 6-pounder anti-tank gun was trained on the tank by a crew of Riflemen led by Sergeant Bray. The Tiger blew it to pieces. Further down the hill in Villers-Bocage itself, the Tiger took out the Honey tanks of the Sharpshooters' Reconnaissance Troop.

The four Cromwell tanks of the regimental headquarters were in the centre of town. One of them, under Major Carr, the Sharpshooters' second in command, went to investigate. When he saw the Tiger advance out of the smoke towards him, he ordered his gunner to fire, but the shell simply bounced off the Tiger's armour. Its reply left the Cromwell a burning wreck and all the crew dead or wounded. The Tiger's next two shots took another two of the RHQ's Cromwells out. Captain Pat Dyas in command of the fourth backed it into a garden and waited. His idea was to knock out Wittmann's Tiger as it trundled past. A 75mm shell could not penetrate the armour-plating on the front or side of the Tiger, but it could jam the turret or knock a track off. But Dyas's gunner had got out of the tank to take a leak shortly before the Tiger appeared and the radio operator did not have time to climb into his seat before the Tiger had passed them. Nevertheless, once the new gunner was in place, Dyas ordered his driver to follow Wittmann's Tiger, in the hope of damaging it with a shot at its more thinly armoured rear. However, when Wittmann reached the end of the street, he met a modified Sherman tank with a 17-pounder gun under the command of Sergeant Lockwood. Wittmann loosed off a shot at him, demolishing a shop behind the Sherman. Lockwood replied, but his shell bounced off the angled facets of the Tiger's turret. Wittmann quickly turned and fled back up the main street running into Dyas in his Cromwell. Dyas found himself facing not the Tiger's thinly armoured rear, but its heavily clad front. Two 75mm shells simply bounced off. Wittmann's reply – one 88mm – hit the Cromwell's turret, killing the wireless operator-turned-gunner and blowing Dyas out of the tank. The driver was cut down by machine-gun fire as he tried to make his escape.

Using a radio that was still functioning in another of the wrecked tanks, Dyas warned Cranley that the Tiger was coming back his way. Cranley replied that he too was under attack. But before they could continue their conversation, a burst of machine-gun fire from the retreating Tiger sent Dyas leaping for cover. After hiding briefly in a pigsty, Dyas was led by a small girl to B Squadron at the west end of the town. There he told Major Aird that, with Cranley cut off and Carr either dead or seriously wounded, he had better take over command of the regiment.

Half an hour later the rest of Wittmann's company arrived on the hill. The four Tigers destroyed the remains of A Squadron and machine-gunned anyone who moved. Then the infantry moved to round up survivors and take them as prisoners of war. The only man to escape was Captain Christopher Milner of A Company, 1st Rifle Brigade. He had made a dash into an orchard. A German spotted him, but he gave his pursuer the slip by climbing a tree. He made good his escape under the cover of a British bombardment of the position. During the night he worked his way around Villers-Bocage, avoiding both Germans and Allied sentries with itchy trigger fingers. At dawn he met up with 5th Royal Tank Regiment to the south-west of the town.

Wittmann caught up with his company and returned to the centre of town with two other Tigers and a Panzer MkIV. This time the British were ready for him. The 1st/7th Queens had entered the town about 1000 and set up an anti-tank gun. Major Aird, now in command of the Sharpshooters, had sent Lieutenant Cotton off to the south to try and skirt round to relieve Cranley avoiding the main street. But he had run into some Germans and a tricky railway embankment and had been forced to return to the town centre. Aware of the danger his troop was in, he hid his tanks in side streets, hoping to get a flanking shot of the Tigers in a short range. Knowing that each tank would have only one chance, he got his men to sight their guns down the barrel using a mark on the wall on the opposite side of the main street. Then he waited.

Driving straight into this ambush, Wittmann's Tiger was put out of action by the Queens' anti-tank gun, though Wittmann and his crew escaped. A modified Sherman with a 17-pounder gun, under the command of Sergeant Bramall, knocked out a second Tiger. The third was caught in a small street to the south and destroyed. Having missed the MkIV with its first shot, Corporal Horne's tank pulled out into the main street and disabled the tank with a shot up its vulnerable back end.

But this was by no means the end of the battle. The Tiger tanks of 1 Company of 101st SS Heavy Tank Battalion turned up, along with a few MkIV tanks from Panzer Lehr and infantry from 2nd Panzer Division. Villers-Bocage became the site of a ferocious battle. As the afternoon wore on, it became clear that the Germans were happy to pour more men in to take the town. At 2000, the order was given for the British to withdraw. They fell back to the high ground near Amayé to the west of the town and did not re-enter Villers-Bocage for two months.

The following dawn the Germans attacked, but were held off by artillery fire, then fled when the Queens counter-attacked. However, that night it was decided that the 22nd Armoured Brigade should withdraw. To cover their retreat, Villers-Bocage was bombed flat.

As it became apparent that the 7th Armoured Division's attempt to cut off the Panzer Lehr Division had failed, the 151st Brigade of 50th Division was ordered to continue the Division's frontal assault. The 1st Battalion of the Durham Light Infantry were to take the village of Lingèvres, supported by A Squadron of the 4th/7th Dragoon Guards, while 6th DLI took Verrières with B Squadron. The attack began at 1015 on 14 June, D+8. There was little time to prepare. Their commanding officer Lieutenant-Colonel Humphrey Wood only had time to for one night of reconnaissance.

The 9th DLI had fought both in North Africa and Sicily, but they had yet to see action in Normandy. Since they had landed they had only sustained one casualty, a sergeant who had drowned on the beach. They were now about to suffer a great many more. The 901st Panzergrenadier Regiment defending Lingèvres had cleared the approaches to the village and had sited machine-guns so that their crossfire would turn them into killing zones.

The battalion would advance in a box formation with A Company leading on the left, followed by B Company, and C Company followed by D on the right. At 1015, they emerged from the woods about a mile north of the Lingèvres as six field regiments, three medium regiments and one heavy regiment – all the artillery within range – began pounding the village. Overhead, Typhoons poured rockets down on the defenders.

As the Durhams reached the woods at the northern side on the village, the artillery bombardment began to roll forward. Almost immediately two German tanks opened fire and A Squadron went after them. Machine guns began to pour withering fire on the advancing infantry causing heavy casualties. Two forward artillery observers were killed. A Company lost all its officers and its advance stalled. Wood ordered B Company up to take over the advance, but quickly it lost all but one of its officers. He then ordered D Company up to press on into the village, while Wood himself aimed to extricate A and B Companies so they could follow D and C around to the right. But before he had a chance to do that, he was killed by a mortar.

Major John Mogg took over command and pushed forward with D and C Companies and the Shermans. They spotted an anti-tank gun in the woods ahead, but a burst from a Sherman's Browning machine-gun set the gun crew to flight. The Durhams reached the village with the Shermans a little way behind. A Squadron's commanding officer Major Goldsmid sent the 4th Troop, under Lieutenant Alastair Morrison, into the village itself to support the infantry, while Captain John Stirling was to take the reserve troop around to the north-west of the village to fend off any attack from that direction.

Inside the village, the Durhams were taking casualties from German mortars. The 901st Panzergrenadier Regiment seemed determined to hold on to Lingèvres and fought house by house, street by street. As they were pushed back, they called in German artillery whose high-explosive shell burst in the air above the village. Casualties collected at the church and a Bren-gun carrier ferried the wounded out, until it was hit by a shell, killing the driver and all on board. At the east of the village, Sergeant Harris saw tanks and he took out a Panther with his 17-pounder gun. Slowly the German infantry were driven out.

By this time Major Mogg had arrived in the village to take charge of the battle. D Company were sent to defend the road to Tilly. C Company held the Longraye road leading south, while the remains of A and B Companies were held in reserve. After liaising with Morrison, Mogg set out to find Major Ken Swann, the artillery commander, to draw up plans for the artillery support needed to knock out any German counter-attack. Then he stationed the battalion's anti-tank guns along all the roads that led in and out of the village. Almost immediately, the two anti-tank guns deployed on the Longraye road were destroyed and their crews killed. Then Sergeant Harris reported seeing a tank approaching from the direction of Tilly. It was a Sherman, but it was followed closely by a German Panther. Harris ordered his gunner, Trooper MacKillop, to fire. He hit the Panther disabling but not destroying it. Mogg himself took a PIAT anti-tank gun and blew up the tank, though the crew escaped.

Another Panther was spotted in a barn on the Longraye road. The Durhams' anti-tank platoon leader Lieutenant Ken Whittaker and Major Goldsmid did a recce and saw one of the German crew standing by the tank, shaving. They decided to attack it simultaneously with a PIAT and a tank. But the PIAT misfired and, while three shells from a Sherman destroyed the barn, the Panther emerged unscathed. With one shot, it disabled the Sherman, fatally wounding the tank commander Corporal Johnson. The radio operator, Lance Corporal Draper, got out and took cover, before he realised that the Sherman's turret was in a position that stopped the driver, Trooper Dagley, getting out. In full sight of the enemy, Draper ran back to the tank, climbed in it and turned the gun so the driver could get out. Then he clambered down to the front of the tank, opened the driver's hatch, pulled Dagley out and carried the badly wounded trooper to safety, though he died a few minutes later. Throughout this reckless rescue, the Germans did not fire on

Draper. He believes this was because they were regular Wehrmacht troops, not soldiers from the ruthless SS formations that were operating in the area at the time.

Several German attempts to retake the village were seen off by artillery fire and Captain Stirling managed to take out a German Panther with three well-aimed 75mm shells from his Sherman. They hit it in the side, just below the turret and it began to burn. The Panther was at the rear of a column of four, which headed east into the village. Harris and MacKillop finished off the other three with their 17-pounder. In all six Panthers had been taken out during the battle, though 9th DLI paid the price, losing 248 men, including twenty-two officers. Nevertheless, they had reason to celebrate. A crate of champagne was found on the back of one of the Panthers and the Durhams toasted their success.

9

OMAHA BEACH

OMAHA BEACH was far from ideal as the site for an amphibious landing. Its 7,000 yards of sand and shingle were overlooked by a hundred-foot escarpment which provided the enemy with a natural fortress. But it was vital that Omaha Beach was taken so that the American forces landing on Utah Beach to the west could join up with the British forces landing to the east to form one continuous beachhead.

Omaha Beach had other disadvantages. It was crescent-shaped, allowing guns along the top of the bluff to concentrate their fire on the troops landing below. The bluff itself was cut up by five wooded ravines or draws which provided the only exits from the beach and the Germans concentrated their firepower down these draws. Strong offshore currents created sand bars and gullies that were exposed at low tide and created difficulties for the landing craft and vehicles coming ashore. To these natural hazards the Germans had added three bands of obstacles their own. Near the low-water mark there were iron structures about ten feet high with Teller anti-tank mines on their uprights. Above those were two rows of wooden poles driving into the sand at a shallow angle, carrying a mine or shell on the tip. Then about halfway up between the low-water mark and the high-water mark were rows of 'hedgehogs': two or three pieces of angled steel joined in the middle, which could puncture the hull of a landing craft.

Mines had been laid on the shingled embankment under the bluff along with improvised booby traps hidden in great coils of barbed wire. Along the top of the bluff were a series of strongpoints which overlooked the draws. Although some of the concrete emplacements had yet to be finished, these strongpoints were well-protected. In them there would be one artillery piece, a 50mm cannon and ten machine-guns manned by a thirty-strong platoon. Overlooking Omaha Beach there were eight concrete bunkers containing heavy 88mm or 75mm guns, sixty light artillery guns, thirty-five small artillery pieces in pill boxes and eighteen anti-tank guns. One central strongpoint also had automatic flame throwers. Between the strongpoints there were infantry trenches with at least eighty-five machine-guns. To the rear there were forty pits housing rocket launchers and mortar positions. Communications between these defences were good and all this fire power could be directed by one man in the central strongpoint overlooking the beach. However, there was one weakness to this defence: shells had to be brought up to the gun emplacements by truck and these had been targeted in air attacks and naval bombardments. While the invasion was being planned, the defences on Omaha Beach were manned by 716th Coastal Defence Division. This division was made up mainly of Slavs and Poles. It was undermanned and its morale was low. But the week before D-Day, elements of the 352nd Infantry Division which had seen action on the Eastern Front had been moved up.

At the western end of Omaha was a formidable German battery, codenamed Maisey, on top of the 100-foot cliff at Pointe du Hoc. Both Omaha and Utah beaches were in range of the six 155mm guns there. It was manned by 210 men: eighty-five artillery men and 125 infantry. Of the 300 enemy installations in the American sector, the destruction of Maisey was given top priority. Bombed by the RAF and the USAAF, and shelled by the 14-inch guns of the USS *Texas*, Pointe du Hoc was hit by more than 10,000 tons of high explosives – the equivalent explosive power of the atomic bomb dropped on Hiroshima. It had little effect, though the bombing and shelling cratered the beach below the cliff, presenting new difficulties to the 2nd Battalion of the US Army Rangers who landed there to knock out Maisey. Another problem was that the Pointe du Hoc looked very much like Pointe et Raz de la Percee, another 100-foot cliff lying closer to Vierville-sur-Mer and Omaha Beach. The Rangers were halfway through their run in, in the twilight, when the commander of the 200-man assault force Colonel James E. Rudder spotted that they were heading for the wrong Pointe. Struggling to reach the right one against the current and tide made them thirty-eight minutes late. This meant they arrived in the daylight and lost the element of surprise. However, the battery's infantry defence was deployed at the rear of the installation as the Germans had not been expecting an attack from the sea.

The Rangers had been trained by the British Royal Marine Commandos in Scotland, where they practised coastal assaults against cliffs, and when they were sent south in April ready for embarkation, they got in more practise on the cliffs around Swanage in Dorset and on the Isle of Wight. They had ten specially modified LCAs with rockets that fired grappling hooks attached to climbing ropes and rope ladders. The craft also carried hand-held rocket devices and lightweight ladders that the Rangers were trained to assemble as they climbed. They also had four amphibious trucks fitted with 100-foot ladders, provided by the London Fire Brigade, with a pair of Lewis guns attached to the top.

The LCAs were launched twelve miles from shore in poor sea conditions. One of the supply boats sank, drowning all but one of its crew. The other supply boat had to jettison half its load to stay afloat. Twenty men and the company commander were rescued when another craft went down. The commanding officer Captain 'Duke' Slater insisted that his company be re-equipped and taken to the beaches, but his men were so numb from the cold water of the Channel they were ordered back to England by the ship's physician. The remaining LCAs were only kept afloat by the men bailing with their helmets. When Colonel Rudder spotted they were heading for the wrong Pointe and altered course, one of the Royal Navy escorts thought he was trying to abort the mission and tried to run him down, though soon realised the mistake. The assault force then had to travel four kilometres along the coastline under heavy fire. One of the escorts was holed beneath the waterline and sank, and one of the amphibious trucks was hit by 20mm cannon fire. More of the LCAs foundered a hundred yards or so from the shore, but most of the men made it to the beach. Only four of the landing craft actually made it to the shore, arriving at 0708 hours, instead of 0630 as planned.

The delay in hitting the beaches meant that the eight sixty-five-man companies from the 2nd and 5th Rangers standing by to support Colonel Rudder did not get the signal to join the assault until the main force hit Omaha Beach. In that case, the plan was for them to divert to the western end of the beach and move overland to join up with Rudder. It was estimated that it would take them until noon to arrive at Pointe de Hoc this way. They did arrive at noon – two days later.

The delay meant that the Germans were ready for Rudder's men. They rained down rifle fire, machine-gun fire, mortars and hand grenades. The Rangers found themselves pinned down at the foot of the cliff and were rapidly being cut to pieces. However, they were greatly encouraged by the bravery of Colonel Travis Trevor, a British commando who had supervised their training and had come along for the ride.

The USS *Satterlee* moved in and engaged the pillbox on the top of the Pointe. Although the naval gunfire had cleared some of the defenders off the clifftop, others continued to throw grenades and rake the Rangers making the dash across the thirty metres of shingle at the bottom of the cliff with machine-gun fire. In the midst of this gun battle, the Rangers had to fire their rockets to get lines up to the top of the cliff and assemble their ladders. The rockets firing the grappling hooks fell short because the ropes they carried were wet and heavy. When a grappling iron did attach itself, the wet and muddy ropes were as slippery as if they had been greased and some men made it halfway up, only to find themselves sliding back down again. The Germans managed to cut some of the ropes. Others tossed grenades over the edge onto the men who were climbing up, but the Rangers had the foresight to tie bits of fuse to the grappling hooks, lighting them before firing the rocket. Seeing the burning fuse, the Germans thought that the grappling hook was some sort of explosive device and kept back.

The amphibious trucks could not get in close enough to use their ladders, partly because bomb and shell damage prevented them from mounting a rocky ledge at the base of the cliff. But Ranger Sergeant William Stivison extended his ladder anyway, climbed to the top and fired at the enemy while he swayed to and fro as waves hit the truck.

At 0728 the naval fire control party reached the top of the cliff and established communications with the fleet. *Satterlee* and USS *McCook* began picking off enemy positions. One gun was blown up and another was knocked off the cliff. The accuracy of the naval artillery support saved many Rangers' lives.

Those who made it to the top of the cliff found shelter in shell and bomb craters. By 0745 all the Rangers were up the cliff and Colonel Rudder established his command post near a destroyed anti-aircraft emplacement. The Rangers had been trained to operate independently and small parties went out after snipers and what remained of the German garrison. A dozen Rangers went to blow up the main guns, but were caught up in a German counterattack. Only one survived. Another twelve Rangers and a mortar team went to avenge them. They were caught by artillery fire and sustained heavy casualties.

By 0830, a party of Rangers had fought their way through to the road from Vierville to Grandcamp, where they established a defensive perimeter and a roadblock. Then they began clearing the bunkers. But they found the emplacements empty. Three days before, the guns had been moved out to protect them from the heavy Allied bombing, leaving telegraph poles in their place. But soon after 0900, a patrol found them in an orchard the other side of the Vierville-Grandcamp road, about 200 yards south of the batteries. They were set up in a well-camouflaged battery, ready to fire on Utah Beach. The Rangers set about smashing the gun sights and traversing mechanisms and destroying the guns with thermite grenades.

The Rangers' objective had now been achieved, but this did not halt the Germans' counter-attacks. Rudder's men were also harassed by a machine-gun position to the east of the Pointe throughout the morning, until naval gunfire blew that section of the clifftop into the sea. By that time the shore-fire-control party was knocked out and artillery support was directed by a bulky World War I-vintage Aldis lamp Lieutenant James Eikner had brought along. Rudder himself was injured when a machine-gun bullet went right through his left leg and he was knocked of his feet by a shell from the British cruiser HMS *Glasgow*, which hit his command post, killing Captain Jonathan Harwood, wounding Lieutenant Kenneth Norton and turning the survivors yellow. The *Glasgow*'s shell had been a coloured marker. Undaunted, Rudder fought on. By noon, the Germans had called in their reserves and Rudder asked for reinforcements. None were available and the only fresh manpower they got were three paratroopers from the 101st Airborne who had somehow made it through the German lines.

By 2100 that evening, a third of the Rangers were wounded or killed and they were running low on ammunition. Then twenty-three of the men from the 5th Rangers turned up. They had been separated from the rest of the battalion on Omaha Beach. When no one else appeared at the rendezvous point, they fought their way through to the Pointe, capturing twenty Germans on the way.

Food was running low too. Private Salva Maimone spotted some cows and milked one of them. But the milk was bitter; the cow had been eating onions which flavoured its milk.

That night, the Germans counter-attacked three times. Finally they broke through the Rangers' perimeter and Rudder was forced to withdraw to a defensive position just 200 yards wide. By the next morning they were out of food and there were less than a hundred men left who could fight. Using Eikner's Aldis lamp, they called for help. USS *Harding* sent a boat to collect the wounded, but it was damaged when it hit the beach. At midday, another boat turned up, bringing ammunition and food. This gave the Rangers new fight and, with close air and naval support, they managed to force the Germans back south of the N13 and they formed a new defensive line along the Aure river. But it was only on the following day that the road from Vierville was cleared and the Rangers' position was relieved, and at 1130 on 8 June Old Glory was raised on Pointe du Hoc. Rudder's men had overrun a fortified garrison, held off five counter-attacks and suffered both enemy artillery and friendly fire. Rudder himself had been injured a second time by shards of concrete blown off a bunker by US naval gunfire. In all, his assault force suffered 70 per cent casualties.

While the Rangers had been fighting on Pointe du Hoc, Omaha Beach itself had seen some ferocious fighting. The beach lay three miles to the east of the Pointe. Things had begun badly there too. At 0540, H-50, thirty-two amphibious tanks from two companies of the 741st Tank Battalion were launched over ten miles out to sea. There was a heavy swell with three to four foot waves. Given the conditions, the tanks were launched too far out. Their flotation screens were simply swamped or pounded by the waves until they gave way. Twenty-seven of the tanks sank. Of their 135 crewmen, few survived. The five tanks that did get ashore fared little better. Three fell victim to German anti-tank guns almost immediately. The amphibious trucks carrying 105mm field guns also sank, so the assault troops were left with practically no artillery support.

The naval bombardment on Omaha started at 0550. Soon after the German batteries began their reply, though Maisey on the Pointe du Hoc was notably silent. At 0600, 480 B-24 Liberator bombers dropped 1,285 tons of bombs. These were aimed at thirteen specific targets. But the cloud ceiling was low, visibility was poor and the bombs were dropped late. Some landed as much as three miles inland, leaving the beach defences unscathed. When the naval bombardment finished at 0625, 3,000 rounds had been fired, again to little effect. British LCTs had also launched a fusillade of 5-inch rockets, but most of them fell short.

Having seen the fate of the 741st's tanks, the Navy Lieutenant in charge of the 743rd's decided to take them into shore. B Company, which landed opposite the Vierville draw, were soon lost to the fire from the German defences there. But A and C Companies landed successfully. They were soon followed by the assault troops in their LCAs.

Each landing craft carried thirty-one men and one officer. Each had six riflemen in the bow carrying an M-1 rifle and ninety-six rounds of ammunition, a four-man wire-cutting team carrying M-1s, a demolition team with TNT charges and Bangalore torpedoes at the ready, two two-man machine-gun teams carrying Browning automatic rifles, two bazooka teams, a four-man mortar team carrying a 60mm mortar and fifteen to twenty mortar rounds, a flame-thrower team, a medic and a section commander in the rear, along with the coxswain. A sergeant or senior NCO was the last to leave the landing craft to make sure that everyone else had left. Soldiers wore clothing impregnated with chemicals to guard against gas attacks and an assault jacket with built-in packs. Each man carried his weapon, five grenades, half a pound of TNT, a gas mask, a life preserver, six packs of rations, a canteen, a first aid kit, a knife, an entrenching tool and any other specialist equipment his job required. When fully equipped, an infantry man carried between sixty and ninety pounds, depending on the type of weapon he carried. Many also carried cigarettes, extra socks and other non-essential items. However, every extra pound made it harder to cross the beach under fire. The boats were arranged in sections of six with each section carrying a company, whose headquarters group would come in with the second wave at 0700.

Of the first wave, only the 16th Infantry Regiment of the 1st Division had combat experience, both in the Western Desert and Sicily. As they jumped down as much as twelve feet into the pitching landing craft sometime before dawn, most men who had no experience of amphibious assaults comforted themselves with the thought that everything would be all right. Those who had assaulted a beach before were less sanguine. The ride from ship to shore took two to three hours. In the heavy seas the men were soaked and cold before they reached the beaches, leaving trigger fingers numb. Almost everyone suffered from seasickness. Most regretted the heavy breakfast of eggs and bacon they had eaten before leaving the transport ship. They had been issued with anti-seasickness pills, but few took them, fearing they would make them drowsy. At least ten landing craft sank. Once in the water, few men survived. The weight of the equipment strapped to them quickly dragged them to the bottom. The men on other boats could do nothing to save them as they were forbidden to stop on their run-in.

Once the naval bombardment stopped, the 800 German defenders returned to their positions and prepared to engage the enemy. They were not stunned and disorganised as the D-Day planners had hoped. The fortifications were undamaged and, in the sector of the beach assaulted by the 16th Regimental Combat Team at least, there was little tank support.

The Germans waited until the first wave of forty-eight landing craft reached the shoreline, where they were confronted by a solid wall of obstacles. Then the Germans unleashed heavy artillery, mortar and machine-gun fire. Survivors recalled the firing being so heavy that running out onto the beaches was akin to committing suicide. But they had no choice.

The German defences had been left unscathed by the air and artillery attacks and the battle-hardened veterans of the 352nd gave courage to the green troops of the 716th. From the eighty-five machine-gun posts and numerous strongpoints along the bluff, the Germans rained down intense fire on the invaders. It was easy for the German machine-gunners to concentrate their fire on the landing ramp of an LCA as it hit the shore. It was bound to drop at any moment, exposing thirty men huddled together – the perfect target. Soon the water was choked with the dead and wounded, and new landing craft coming had no choice but to run over them. Inside the LCAs, the assault troops would hear the bullets bouncing off the metal ramp, knowing that the moment they hit the beach that protection would be snatched away from them.

The heavy fire caused some of the coxswains to drop their ramps too early, dropping the troops into water that covered their heads. Others hit unexpected sandbars and left men stranded too far from the beach to wade ashore. This meant that valuable equipment had to be discarded and men arrived at the beach without weapons and too exhausted to advance. Those who kept hold of their guns found them jammed with wet sand. Some of those too tired to move drowned when the tide came in.

Thirty-two 'Stonewallers' from the 116th RCT of the 29th Division were wiped out to a man as they left their LCA. To avoid the machine-gun fire coming in through the ramp opening, some men jumped over the sides of the landing craft, only to drown. Three LCAs of A Company of the 116th RCT were hit by concentrated fire and suffered appalling casualties. Other LCAs were blown up when they ran into mines or were hit by shells. The other two LCAs of A Company had not even made it to the beaches. Within twenty minutes, the Company lost sixty per cent of its men and was left 'inert, leaderless and almost incapable of action', according to one surviving private.

The strong wind and tide had pushed the landing craft well to the east. Some hit the beach a thousand yards from where they were supposed to be and could find no familiar landmarks to orientate themselves. Following the infantry were the engineers. Their larger landing craft were targeted and many destroyed. They were particularly vulnerable as they were full of TNT to clear the mines and beach obstacles. Some sixty per cent of the engineers' equipment was destroyed on Omaha Beach on D-Day.

Ten bulldozers were lost on the run-in. Another three were shot up on the beach, leaving just three working vehicles. One landing craft, mechanised (LCM) received a direct hit as it approached the beach, detonating the explosives and killing the entire navy team. Only one of an eight-man navy demolition team survived when their heavily laden rubber dingy was hit by shrapnel. Once on the beaches the engineers were confronted with worse problems. There were few tanks to give them covering fire and their task was to blow up the beach obstacles that many of the infantry were using as cover. Several engineers were killed when bullets hit the explosives they were planting. One team preparing a thirty-metre gap was wiped out when a mortar set off their primer.

Those infantrymen who made it across the beach found shelter behind a small bank of shale, but to get there they had to run the gauntlet of murderous crossfire from the German machine-gunners. To make that sprint, most men abandoned their heavy packs, so they arrived at the shale without the equipment they needed to move on. The men who huddled there were badly disorientated and disorganised. Few had any idea where the rest of their unit was and they received no orders as all their radio equipment had been lost. Some tended to the wounded. Others searched for their unit leader, cleaned their weapons or simply stared out into space. They were trapped. Ahead of them lay a minefield; beyond that the bluff. Behind them more and more men were being landed. The men sheltering behind the shale had to watch as those that followed them were butchered: blown up and cut to pieces by machine-gun fire. Anyone who attempted to make it down to the water and drag a wounded buddy to safety was cut down.

Even though what remained of the forward fire controllers had no way of communicating with their ships, the navy saw what was happening and saved the day. The destroyers moved in so close that they were hit by German rifle fire. They began pounding the beach defences. This boosted the morale of the troops trapped on the beach and gave the infantry the break they needed.

When the second wave hit at 0700, they expected to find the beaches cleared and move directly inland to their objectives. As it was, most of the beach obstacles were still in place. Only six of the proposed sixteen fifty-metre-wide lanes had been cleared – and only one fully marked. Landing craft sailed up and down the shore looking for a clear place to land. If they did not find one, they nudged their way gingerly through the obstacles, some of which were rigged with mines.

Many were hit by artillery fire in the water and the survival rate was little better than the men in the first-wave boats. Those who made it to the beaches faced a suicidal dash to the sea wall. Finding themselves in the wrong position, some tried to move laterally to the place where they should be, taking heavy casualties on the way. But some units got lucky. Grass on the bluffs to the west of the draw that led up to St Laurent caught fire and smoke obscured the right end of the beach. K Company of the 3rd Battalion of the 116th Infantry made it to their beach exit with only one casualty, a lieutenant who had been stabbed accidentally with a bayonet while still on the landing craft.

But it was soon clear to anyone on the beach that the situation was generally a disaster. A Company from the 116th and C Company from the 2nd Rangers had been cut to pieces and had effectively ceased to exist as fighting units. G and F Companies were scattered and disorganised, having suffered heavy casualties and E Company was disorientated. With the tide coming in, the weak and the wounded were left to drown. Others hid behind the shale or the sea wall, unsure of what to do.

The second wave brought headquarters units and with them General Norman D. Cota, who landed at H+57. Realising the situation was desperate, he exposed himself to enemy fire leading his men over the sea wall. He personally supervised the siting of a BAR (Browning Automatic Rifle) and brought fire to bear on an enemy position. By 0830, the commanders of both the 16th Infantry, Colonel George Taylor, and the 116th Infantry, Colonel Charles D.W. Canham were ashore, along with the assistant division commander, General Willard G. Wyman, but still no one in that sector had advanced off the beach. However, some sort of a command structure was in place and new, make-shift units were formed.

Men gave their lives to cross the minefield, their mutilated corpses marking the path for those who followed. One young officer threw himself down on the ground to clear the last few feet of a minefield for his men, detonating a mine which killed him. His men advanced over him. Slowly the soldiers began making their way towards the bluff.

To the east of the beach, things were particularly confused. Currents and navigational errors had delivered the bulk of the force into a German killing zone where there was not so much as a sea wall for cover. The men had to cross 500 yards of open beach before they could find cover in the sand dunes. There they were pinned down by machine-gun fire from the bluff high above. They were trapped there until Colonel George Taylor turned up at 0830.

Colonel Taylor told his men, 'Two kinds of people are staying on this beach, the dead and those who are going to die. Now let's get the hell out of here.'

Along the beach, ragged bunches of men began to realise that it was better to try and fight their way off the beaches than stay in the Germans' well-planned killing zone. A sergeant shoved a Bangalore torpedo under the wire at the top of the dune and blew a gap in it. Then Colonel Taylor led his men through it. They dashed though a flat area towards the base of the bluff. It was heavily mined and there were many casualties.

By 0900 there were five thousand men on the beach. The situation still looked grim, but between 0900 and 1000 hours, elements of the 16th Infantry managed to find their way to the top of the bluff and, in close, hand-to-hand fighting, they moved along it, clearing German fortifications. A platoon lead by Lieutenant Spaulding attacked a strongpoint that covered the east side of one of the draws. Five machines and an anti-aircraft gun housed in two pillboxes and four concrete shelters covered the beach exit. There was a close exchange of hand grenades and small arms fire. Eventually one German officer and twenty men surrendered. By the time reinforcements arrived on the eastern sector of the beach at 1000, the exit was secure. Even so another twenty-eight landing craft were lost to underwater obstacles.

Thanks to General Cota, the 116th Infantry began to make progress too. He sent a man forward to blow a hole in the wire with a Bangalore torpedo. But the first man through the gap was cut down by German fire and no one seemed eager to follow him. So Cota seized the moment. He ran through the gap and across the road beyond it, then he shouted for his men to follow him. They did and, miraculously, not one of them was hit. They advanced 100 yards through reeds and grass to the base of the bluff. A German trench, which was luckily empty, provided some cover. But at the other end of it they found themselves in a minefield. Nevertheless they headed onwards and upwards, though a number of Cota's men were badly wounded by the anti-personnel mines. However, those who were not wounded were further motivated by a horrendous sight down below. The Germans were machine-gunning their own men who had surrendered to the Americans.

Cota's group reached the top of the bluff at around 0900. The General then split his makeshift unit up into fire teams and sent them to take out a machine-gun that stood between them and the draw at Les Moulins. They then moved around to take Vierville from the rear. There they met other elements of the 116th, who were greeted by Cota walking down the main street twirling his pistols like something out of a Western. Colonel Canham had fought his way up the bluff and met up with Cota in Vierville too. Together they cooked up a plan to get their men off the beaches. Canham would clear the draw at Les Moulins by attacking the Germans from the rear, while Cota would unplug the draw below Vierville where a paved road ran down to the shore.

Cota took just five men with him down the draw. The German positions below them were now coming under fire from the 14-inch guns of the USS *Texas*. Between 1223 and 1230, six shells hit the German fortification. The concussed occupants put up only a token resistance. After a brief firefight, they surrendered to Cota's tiny force. Using the Germans as guides to take him through the minefield, Cota made his way back to the beach where a horrifying scene of destruction met him. Quickly he marshalled some explosives to blow an obstruction in the draw that prevented armour leaving the beach. Soon men and machines were marching up the draw and General Cota made his way east along the beach encouraging other men to move forward.

To the commanders viewing the beaches from offshore, the situation was still far from clear and it was decided to throw the reserves into the battle and at 1045 the 115th Infantry arrived on the beach. Still the exits had not been secured, but the 115th moved up the bluff and took the village of St Laurent, which dominated the road system directly inland. By 1200 there were four major breaches in the German defences. As the afternoon progressed the breaches were widened and American troops began to move inland. However, this could not be seen by those out on the ships. There was little radio communication as seventy-five per cent of the assault force's radios had been lost. General Omar Bradley, in command of the American First Army, considered evacuating the beach and taking his men to the British sector where the landings seemed to have gone more smoothly. When he reported back to SHAEF that the landings on Omaha Beach were a disaster, Eisenhower ordered the Allied air forces to bomb Omaha Beach. The attack was to begin at 1330. Luckily, this could not be done. It would have turned a disastrous situation into a catastrophe.

Fortunately, the German commander General Kraiss was getting similarly inaccurate reports. It seemed to him that the defences at Omaha had held. If Kraiss had sent his reserves that morning, they would probably have been able to push the Americans back into the sea. As it was his reserves were sent out to track down paratroopers, but they found it difficult to move during daylight due to harassment by Allied fighters. And Kraiss decided that, if anything, any spare manpower should be concentrated on the British beaches where the situation seemed more desperate from the German point of view.

At 1600, the 1st Infantry Division commander General Clarence R. Huebner came ashore to direct operations on the beach personally. With him came the artillery that the infantry needed to secure its advances. The 26th Regiment landed at 1930. It was redirected to clear Colleville, behind the beaches occupied by the 16th, and advanced through St Laurent inland to Formigny.

By dark, after a disastrous start to the day on Omaha Beach, fire support was in position and it became clear that the Germans were in no position to counter-attack. At the end of D-Day, the 1st Infantry Division at Omaha Beach controlled a strip of Normandy 10,000 yards wide and 2–3,000 yards deep. It was not much, but it was a foothold. For this tiny piece of land, they had paid with 2,000 casualties.

By midnight, the Vierville draw was secure and the coast road was cut. The 116th Infantry held positions to the west and south of the village. The 2nd and 5th Rangers tried to swing to the west to meet up with their comrades on Pointe du Hoc, but were stopped by German outposts. The 115th Infantry under Colonel Eugene N.

Slappey moved off the beach up the Les Moulins draw but they ran into opposition from Germans occupying the village of St Laurent, which blocked the exit to that draw and another one, a dirt path that led down to the beach. Slappey sent his 1st Battalion around to the south of the village to prevent the German garrison being reinforced, and he sent his other two battalions into the village from the east. They ran into stiff resistance and St Laurent did not fall to the Americans until the next day. To the east Colleville changed hands several times that day, but ended up being held by the Germans that night, though it was virtually encircled. When the Americans had held it earlier that day, due to a communications mix up, the village had been raked by naval gunfire, killing sixty-four men.

German positions on the bluffs were cut off and retreating German troops found themselves falling into ambushes where the GIs took understandably savage revenge. But most of the defenders stayed in place until their ammunition ran out. They had been ordered to do so. The Führer himself had told them not to give up an inch of his murderous empire and Rommel's plan was to stop the invasion cold on the beaches. This was a mistake. Maintaining their positions on the bluff meant that the Germans could go on killing Americans, but could not win the battle. They could not fall back and form up to stage concentrated counter-attacks. Inland was bocage country, but the Germans only managed to stage a piece-meal defensive action there. Although the remaining defenders on the bluff would slow the Allies down and inflict numerous casualties, they were bound to fail in the end as they were receiving no reinforcement while wave after wave of fresh troops were coming in over the beaches.

That is not to say that the Germans were not good soldiers. When an American officer was interrogating a German prisoner about the whereabouts of minefields, the German would only give his name, rank and serial number, as stipulated by the Geneva Conventions. So the American fired his carbine between the German's legs. The

German pointed to his crotch and said, '*Nicht hier*', then pointed to his head and said, '*Hier.*' The interrogator gave up.

Even though they had got up the bluff, it was difficult for the Americans to maintain the momentum of their advance. Troops who had survived the hell of the beaches understandably felt that they had done their job for the day. They wanted a rest. Those who made it into villages found wine and took a drink. However to the west of Vierville, the Rangers determinedly pushed on towards their buddies on Pointe du Hoc.

Once they were off the beaches, the Americans also had to switch to a new style of fighting. Bold leadership worked when soldiers were storming the bluff, but when fighting from hedgerow to hedgerow, those who went boldly ahead got killed. Sheltering behind the ridge of shale or behind a seawall, a soldier could see that he had two choices: advance or die. In bocage country, those who stayed under cover survived.

Vierville itself remained the weakest part of the American line that first night. Its church was taken out by USS Harding after Colonel Canham suspected that its steeple was being used by a German artillery spotter. Many of the churches in Normandy suffered a similar fate.

On Omaha Beach, the American V Corps suffered 2,400 dead, wounded and missing, and put ashore 34,000 troops out of its 55,000 assault force. On D-Day alone, they had a casualty rate of 7.2 per cent, which would normally be considered horrendous, though it was five per cent less than expected. The German losses were only half of the Americans – 1,200 in all – but that was twenty per cent of their defence force, and they had not succeeded in their objective, snuffing out the invasion on the beaches.

The following day, not only did the Americans hold on to their foothold, they expanded it. Then on 8 June, the 'Gooseberries' arrived. These were sixty block ships that were to be sunk off Omaha and Gold beaches to make breakwaters for the two

Mulberry Harbours that were going to be built there. The convoy was assembled in Poole Harbour the evening before D-Day in the berths recently vacated by the troop ships. The following morning they headed at six knots to Area Z – also known as Piccadilly Circus – where the ships of the invasion force had been mustered. At midnight they headed south. It was a dangerous voyage. Although the area used by the invasion force had been swept, the Channel was full of mines and, in the dark, the *Durban* was almost run down by another ship that appeared to be out of control.

The first convoy of blockships were due to be off Omaha Beach at 1230 on 7 June, but before they got there, the enemy launched a counter-attack by sea and air in the Battle of Seine Bay. German E-boats from Cherbourg and R-boats from Le Havre had ventured out into the Channel. An Allied naval force quickly intercepted them and damaged a few before they raced back to port. The Luftwaffe were flying again, although they never seriously challenged Allied air superiority. However, the fact that they were airborne put anti-aircraft teams on the alert and Allied naval gunners accidentally shot at planes carrying airborne reinforcements, downing one Dakota and killing all on board. The Luftwaffe dropped fresh mines. German coastal guns were still blazing away at Allied shipping and the Germans launched attacks with midget submarines, human torpedoes and unmanned motor patrol boats packed with explosives. The aim was to break up the Trout line – the line of Allied ships that bombarded the shore and protected the beaches from an attack from the rear.

The Gooseberries spent the night of 7 June inside the Trout line. The next morning the 'Planter', commanding the operation, directed the ships towards the coast down lanes that had been swept of mines. Each boat had to be positioned exactly before being scuttled. The *Alynbank* was the first to go down. She was towed into position by tugs. But, as she sank, she swung around, pointing her prow at the coast rather than lying parallel to it. There had also been fears that these old ships would not settle on an even keel, so they had been heavily ballasted. In the Alynbank's case it had not worked.

Once each ship was in place, a charge was laid. When it was blown, the ship went down until only its funnel, mast and super-structure were visible above the water. The line of sunken ships broke the swell and to the landward side of it the water was visibly calm. As the last ship was sunk, the Mulberry Harbours' huge con-crete caissons appeared over the horizon. Each weighed around 1,500 tons and were 200ft long, 50ft wide and 60ft high. There were 146 of them. These had to be positioned with extreme accuracy and they could only be sunk in a light wind and a slack tide. These were rare that week, but the tug masters were skilful and held them in position as the seacocks were opened and they sank to the sea floor. In all there was two million tons of floating harbour to be trans-ported across the Channel, costing over £40 million. Each of the Mulberries would enclose two square miles of water – they would be larger than Dover harbour which took two years to build.

Due to the heavy seas in the Channel, forty per cent of the road-way that would carry supplies from the piers to the shore was lost or damaged. The inner floating breakwaters arrived more or less intact and the Mulberry Harbour on Omaha Beach was working by D+5, the British Mulberry at Arromanches, near Gold Beach, was in operation the following day. Up until that time, supplies had been delivered by flat-bottomed coasters that could come right up to the beaches and be unloaded by amphibious trucks. Now deepwater vessels could tie up at the Mulberries' pierhead and be unloaded by a convoy of trucks that drove straight down the floating roadways to the shore.

Even though they were up and working, the Mulberries were far from complete. Work continued on their construction but from 14 June, D+8 to 18 June, the weather deteriorated steadily. One and a half million tons of material was still waiting to be towed across the Channel. The roadway particularly needed to be carried on calm seas. On 18 June, the winds dropped. The barometer was high, the sea calm and twenty-two sections of floating roadway set sail from the Solent, heading for France. They were halfway across the Channel at 0800 next morning when a storm hit. At first it was Force three, then five, then eight. It turned out to be the worst nor'easter for forty years. The tugs continued valiantly on their way but, battered by the waves, the tow ropes snapped. Only one of the twenty two sections reached the coast of France.

At the Mulberry Harbours themselves, all unloading stopped and half-laden ships headed back out to sea, rather than risk being blown onto the shore. Small craft found shelter in the lee of the sunken blockships. Unfortunately, the gale coincided with a spring tide, so the sunken ships did not offer all the protection they did at other times. Many of the boats taking shelter there capsized or were flung onto the shore.

At Omaha Beach, the blockships had been sunk hurriedly and there was a great gap in the middle. This made things easier for shipping, but it allowed in the full force of the gale. Some of the ships were damaged too. They had broken their backs as they sank, and as the high seas scoured sand from underneath them, they settled into the seabed, allowing more of the force of the gale to pass over them. The floating breakwaters broke loose and lashed the caissons. Pounded by the sea, the concrete caissons cracked, crumbled and disintegrated. Vessels sheltering inside the harbour were now exposed to the storm. They crashed into the floating roadways that had sunk. The harbour at Omaha Beach had to be abandoned completely, though parts of it were salvaged and used at Arromanches. The storm had also left 800 craft damaged and beached, but within two weeks 700 of them had been repaired and refloated.

The Mulberry Harbour at Arromanches had been built in shallower and less exposed waters. It was to some degree sheltered by the Calvados reef. Only four of its caissons actually disintegrated. Its floating breakwaters resisted the fifteen-foot waves for thirty hours, before finally breaking loose and drifting ashore. But the harbour itself survived.

The remarkable thing is that, had the invasion been postponed again after 6 June, the next possible dates when it could have taken place were 17 or 18 June. The storm struck on 19 June, by which time the Allied armies would have been on shore without enough ammunition or supplies to fight their way inland or, possibly, even hold the beachhead.

Although the Americans had lost the use of their Mulberry Harbour, their troops were already just three miles outside Cherbourg. At the height of the storm they started their assault on the ditches, wire and minefields that constituted the port's last lines of defence. On 21 June, the Germans refused to surrender. They fought on fanatically for four more days. On 27 June Cherbourg was finally in American hands. A team of Royal Navy frogmen were then called in to clear it of the special K mines the Germans had left. These were explosives set in a block of concrete that were triggered by floating green snag lines that were almost impossible to detect. The idea was that these would wind around a propeller and when the line tightened it would set off the charge, blowing up anything that was above it.

The other great logistical miracle of the invasion was PLUTO – Pipe Line Under the Ocean. To advance quickly out of the beachheads and across northern Europe, huge amounts of petrol would be needed. The Allies had already seen the failure of German advances in the western desert that depended on capturing fuel to maintain their momentum. So the British had another brainwave – pipe gasoline under the sea.

The idea had its origin in 1942, when a thousand miles of pipelines were laid across Britain to carry petrol landed in the safer ports of the west coast to London, the south and the east of the country. If it was possible to pipe petrol right across England, why couldn't it be pumped directly from England to France? Engineers developed a 3-inch-diameter flexible pipe that could be laid from the back of a ship. A pumping station was built on the Isle of Wight. Another was built at Dungeness which would be used to pump petrol to Calais when the front had advanced that far.

Cable-laying coasters had to be modified to carry two-mile coils of piping. Soon after D-Day they set out at five knots, little more than walking pace. Every two miles, they would stop and a second ship would take over. Eventually four pipelines spanned the seventy miles from Southampton Water Terminal to Cherbourg and one million gallons of fuel a day was being pumped across the Channel.

The storm that destroyed the Mulberry Harbour at Omaha Beach also brought the Allies an unexpected benefit, neutralising a secret weapon that could have destroyed the entire invasion. During the war both sides, unknown to each other, had been working on a new kind of mine. Known as the oyster mine, it was triggered by the change in water pressure caused by the wave trough of a ship. Ironically enough, the Germans had caught on to this idea when one of their naval officers, Lieutenant-Commander Fett studied a survey of the English canal system which mentioned that the wave trough of a barge lowered the water pressure beneath it. The Germans developed two types of oyster mines. The acoustic version was armed by the change in water pressure of a ship sailing over it and detonated by the noise of its engines. The magnetic version, again, was armed by the change in water pressure, but detonated by the magnetic variations caused by the hull of the ship.

Although both sides developed such devices, they did not deploy them, because there was no way they could be detected or, effectively swept. That meant, if the other side captured one, they could reproduce them, leaving the side that laid them with no means of defence. However, as the war drew on, the deployment of oyster mines began to favour the Germans, whose fleet was largely confined to port. When it became obvious that the Allies planned an amphibious assault on France, their use became very much to the

German advantage. The plan was to lay them immediately after the Allied troops had hit the beaches. They would destroy the ships bringing supplies to the assault force and deny them any prospect of evacuation. The beleaguered army would be stranded on a hostile coast and the Western Allies would be forced to sue for peace.

Two thousand oyster mines were sent to France on Hitler's orders. A further 2,000 were held back in Germany, then moved to Norway and later Holland, depending on where Operation Fortitude was giving the impression that the invasion was coming. They would be laid only on the specific command of Hitler, but in May 1944 Göring ordered them to be returned to Germany. The last arrived back in Magdeburg just a few days before D-Day. At that time, it was thought that Allied invasion would come on the Atlantic coast, where the water was too deep for the oysters, which sat on the sea floor, to be effective and where they risked being triggered by the swell. A vital part of the mine's pressure detecting system was a rudder bag that was highly perishable and an improved version was about to became available. It was also feared that, if the invasion did come on the Atlantic coast, the oysters stored in Le Mans would be captured before they could be used.

After D-Day the order was given to lay the oysters, but the Allied air forces had spent the first weeks of June bombing all lines of communication between Germany and France, including Magdeburg and other airfields from which the oysters could be flown to the French coast. It took weeks for them to arrive. Meanwhile the E-boats and R-boats working out of Le Havre tried laying conventional mines to prevent the Allies resupplying. On 14 and 15 June, the RAF bombed Le Havre, putting an end to that.

Though the whole invasion area was constantly being swept, from D+10, ships began to go down in large numbers. It was quickly realised that a new kind of mine was being deployed by the Luftwaffe flying low over the area at night to avoid Allied radar and night fighters. Then, on D+14, the Allies got lucky. On the night of

19-20 June, the storm caused the Luftwaffe to drop two oyster mines over land at Luc-sur-Mer. Oyster mines were fitted with detonators, so that they would explode if they hit dry land. One blew up, but there was a fault with the other one and it only blew one end off. It was found by Sub-Lieutenant Young of the Royal Navy Volunteer Reserve who had been sheltering from an air raid in Luc-sur-Mer. Young knew something about mines. He recognised that this was a type not seen before. He also noticed that it had a small bulge that indicated the presence of some sort of photo-electric device. This meant that, if you tried to dismantle it, when you opened the case, light falling on this device would detonate the mine. It was shipped back to England, where Royal Navy mine experts set to work on it. They drilled holes in the casing with a remote-controlled device, then, after dark, finished off disconnecting the firing circuits.

Once they confirmed that it was an oyster mine, the Admiralty ordered all ships in the invasion area to cut their speed to the bare minimum. This reduced the drop in water pressure caused by the trough and had the additional benefit of cutting the ship's engine noise and the change in the magnetic field its moving hull caused. Casualties were dramatically reduced. But the oyster mines still had to be swept. Luckily the heavy swell caused by the storm had activated the pressure part of the mechanism and 500 of the oyster mines exploded harmlessly. With the pressure part of the mechanism activated the mines were easier to detect. Minesweepers could then detonate them. Once again, it seems, luck was on the Allies' side.

10

UTAH BEACH

DUE TO THE WAY the tide runs up the Channel, the first assault was on Utah, the most westerly of the invasion beaches, where, once again things began badly. Aerial reconnaissance had spotted enemy activity off shore on a group of small islands called the Iles St Marcouf. It was thought that the Germans had an observation post or even a gun emplacement there that would threaten the landings on the beach. At 0430 on D-Day, four scouts went ashore from rubber dinghies to mark the beach for Force U, a detachment of 132 men from the 4th and 24th Cavalry Squadrons who would secure the island before the main landings on Utah Beach.

They were carried by four landing craft that arrived in two waves. They found no Germans on the islands. By the time they had discovered this, five men had been killed by mines. The cavalry moved on to Utah Beach itself and were replaced by an anti-aircraft detachment, who sustained a further fourteen casualties that day due to mines and booby traps on the islands.

At 0455, the first of twenty-four waves of landing craft headed for Utah Beach and at 0550 Allied warships began their bombardment of the German fortifications. Then a fleet of bombers dropped over four thousand 250-pound bombs on the enemy positions, which were simultaneously hit by 1,000 rockets. Unlike on Omaha Beach, this bombardment was successful, leaving many of the defenders disorientated and eager to surrender. But that did not mean that the rest of the assault went smoothly.

The plan was for the thirty-two amphibious tanks to land first at 0630, directly the warships had lifted their bombardment. Twenty LCAs would follow carrying thirty men each from the 2nd Battalion,

8th Infantry. Ten of them were targeted at the German strongpoint at Les Dunes de Varreville at the north end of the beach. A second wave of thirty-two boats would arrive five minutes later, carrying the 1st Battalion, 8th Infantry, along with naval demolition teams and combat engineers. Ten minutes after that landing craft would land regular Sherman tanks on the beach, along with bulldozer tanks. Two minutes after that the fourth wave would hit, carrying detachments of the 237th and 299th Engineer Combat Battalions.

Nothing in this plan worked out. Everyone landed at least a kilometre south of where they were supposed to be. Most were late. This was partially due to the heavy seas and smoke obscuring the beach, but the main problem was that three of the four boats controlling the assault were lost to mines out to sea before the run-in even began. The sole remaining control craft decided that, to make up for lost time, the amphibious tanks should be launched just three kilometres out from shore, rather than the planned five kilometres. However, in the confusion, they headed for the wrong beach.

The LCAs carrying the assault troops were supposed to stay behind the tanks. They sailed past them, but a strong current pushed them even further to the left. The first landing craft to hit the beach carried E Company of the 2nd Battalion, 8th Regiment. It was also carrying a VIP. Despite his age – fifty-six – and his poor physical condition – he had had a heart attack and walked with a stick – the assistant division commander of the 4th Infantry Division, Brigadier-General Theodore Roosevelt Jnr, son of the former president and cousin of the current one, had managed to persuade his commanding officer Major-General Raymond O. Barton to let him go ashore in the first wave on the grounds that it would be good for the troops' morale.

'They'll figure that if a general is going in, it can't be that rough,' Roosevelt said.

He had been lucky. Instead of landing opposite the heavy German fortifications as planned, they had landed opposite a battery that had been so badly battered by the naval bombardment that the defenders had been driven from it and offered only token small-arms fire from a trench just behind the sea wall. Once the GIs had waded ashore and covered the 200 yards of open beach, they found Germans ready to surrender.

Around 0640, the strongpoint at Les Dunes de Varreville began to turn their fire on the beachhead, but they were too far away to be accurate. By then two Shermans had arrived and began firing back. Roosevelt had a conference in a shell hole with Colonel James Van Fleet, commanding officer of the regiment. They worked out that they were in the wrong place – ironically, in exactly the spot Van Fleet wanted to land. They had a decision to make. Should they move the entire landing force a mile northwards up the beach and go back to the original plan, or strike inland from where they were as assault troops were already crossing the sea wall and the engineers were clearing obstacles from the beach? Roosevelt was famed for saying, 'We'll start the war from right here.'

Van Fleet disputes this. He said that he made the decision, saying, 'We've caught the enemy at a weak point, let's take advantage of it.'

Whichever was the case, it was Roosevelt who made the decision stick. As second-in-command of the 4th Infantry Division, he had the authority to order the succeeding waves to land where they had landed, without anyone countermanding his orders. This flexibility won the day at Utah Beach and General Roosevelt was awarded the Medal of Honour.

By the time the second wave arrived, the Germans had recovered a little from the pounding they had received. The strongpoint at St Marie du Mont opened up with machine-guns, hitting the lead group of the second wave. German mortars began firing at the craft out at sea. But this only succeeded in giving away their position and they were soon silenced by naval gunfire. The German strongpoint managed to get its bomb-damaged 88mm gun working. It loosed off one shell which damaged an amphibious tank.

The Germans were taken by surprise by the Allies' amphibious tanks. Lieutenant Arthur Jahnke, the twenty-three-year-old veteran of the Eastern Front who commanded the strongpoint at St Marie du Mont, thought he must be hallucinating as a result of concussion from the bombardment when he first saw them. Then he realised that they were the Allies' secret weapon. But the Germans had a secret weapon of their own. This was the Goliath tank, a small remote-controlled tracked vehicle packed with 224 pounds of explosives. Jahnke gave the order to send the Goliaths out against the amphibious tanks, only to find that their delicate radio control mechanisms had been damaged by the bombardment.

Despite the determination of its defenders, the naval bombardment of St Marie du Mont was too much for them and the strongpoint was overrun. Jahnke himself was captured in a makeshift dugout shooting at Americans with his rifle. A tank blasted his position with 75mm cannon and a GI dragged him out. Jahnke tried to make a grab for the GI's machine-gun, but the American calmly pushed his hand aside and told him to take it easy. With the other survivors he was marched down to the beach with his hands on his head and waited to be taken out to Allied ships. Although the resistance of coastal defenders soon ceased, the beach came under continued attack by artillery further inland until D+13, Jahnke himself being wounded by shrapnel from an incoming German shell as he waited in the POW enclosure on the beach.

Despite the shelling, demolition teams began clearing the beaches. This was done by Naval Seabee (combat demolition units) men. They were older than most men on the beach on D-Day. Most of them were miners from the western states who were experts with explosives. They also had to be good swimmers. They cleared the obstacles closest to the sea first, as they would be the first to be covered by the incoming tide. This presented a problem as infantrymen fresh off the LCAs liked to take cover behind the obstacles before making their run across the open beaches. They also had problems with General Roosevelt who liked to walk about on the beach waving his stick, refusing to take cover. But within an hour the teams had cleared eight fifty-yards gaps in the obstacles and were beginning to pick off those in between.

Next they blasted holes in the anti-tank sea wall, leaving the bulldozer tanks to clear away the debris. Then they moved on to deal with the gun emplacements, only to find Germans still in them, though they were eager to surrender or flee across the causeways.

Succeeding waves hitting the beach were shelled by 88mm guns inland, but to little effect as the Germans had no forward observers. So many men began to build up on the beaches that the engineers found themselves forced to move inland. Just inland there were fields of S-mines, commonly known as Bouncing Betties. These mines bounced up into the air before they exploded to devastating effect. They caused numerous casualties on Utah Beach that day. A number of tanks were also hit and disabled by mines.

Advanced elements of the American infantry quickly made their way inland across the causeways directly behind the beaches and came under mortar fire. They also found that bridges in the causeways had been wired for demolition, but they were not blown. Although there was sporadic resistance by German snipers, most of the defenders, when challenged, gave up without a fight.

At 1110, scouts at the western edge of the flooded area behind the beaches saw a helmet behind a bush. Not knowing whether the owner was an American or a German, they set off an orange flare. Two men stood up. They were wearing the Stars and Stripes on their shoulders. The 4th Division had linked up with the 101st. The 101st had already taken Pouppeville, killing forty Germans. Together they secured St Marie du Mont.

Landing so far to the south was a problem for the 12th Infantry Regiment as their first objective was St Martin de Varreville, which lay to the north. The causeway leading inland from the beach was jammed with tanks, trucks and troops, and the next exit was coming under fire from four 155mm guns at St Marcouf. The commanding officer of the 12th Infantry, Colonel Russell 'Red' Reeder made the decision to have his men wade though the flooded area to St Marie de Varreville. According to aerial reconnaissance, there was just eighteen inches of water in the irrigation ditches. Elsewhere it was only supposed to be ankle-deep. But when the men set out, they soon found that it was waist deep in the flood fields and, in the irrigation ditches, it was over a man's head. Brave souls would swim across and throw a rope back to haul the rest of the unit across. For nearly two kilometres the troops struggled on in constant danger of drowning. One slip and the weight of their equipment would pull them down. Men cursed the navy for trying to drown them on their way to the beaches and cursed the army for trying to drown them when they were ashore. The Germans' sporadic sniper fire was merely an irritant.

When the 1st Battalion reached high ground, General Roosevelt, who had hitched a ride on the hood of a jeep, turned up.

'Let's go up to the front,' he said to the 1st Battalion's commanding officer, Lieutenant Colonel Charles 'Chuck' Jackson.

'This is the front, sir,' said Colonel Jackson. And he pointed out the two leading scouts of A Company some fifty yards ahead.

'Let's go talk to them,' said Roosevelt. They did and Roosevelt's pep talk reinvigorated the battalion. By late afternoon, they had hooked up with the 82nd Airborne at St Germain de Varreville, St Martin de Varreville and Chef du Pont.

Much of the credit for the speed of the American advance belonged to the navy. Every time the 4th Division ran into enemy armour, they called back to the warships for artillery support. The USS *Nevada* fired so many salvos that the paint peeled off the gun barrels leaving the steel burnished blue underneath. Normally, they kept the empty shell cases for reloading, but these hindered the movement of the gun turrets so they were thrown overboard. The sheer force of the volleys distorted the superstructure of the ship.

Doors fell off. Bulkheads shifted. Light fittings broke and many men reported hearing loss.

By the middle of the afternoon, Utah Beach had been cleared of obstacles and a small city had taken shape. There was a steady stream of men badly wounded by Bouncing Betties being stretchered back to the beaches, while overhead gliders brought in more reinforcements. There was no doubt in anyone's mind that Utah Beach was secure. Next day they would set off to take Montebourg, seal off the Cotentin peninsula and go on to take Cherbourg.

American losses on Utah were comparatively light. The 12th Regiment suffered sixty-nine casualties, mainly caused by mines, particularly Bouncing Betties. The 8th and the 22nd Regiments suffered 106 wounded and twelve dead. In all, the 4th Division lost twenty times more men during training following the disaster in Lyme Bay.

The landing on Utah Beach was one of the major successes of D-Day. The paratroopers' role was vital, confusing the enemy, holding the western exits to the beaches and preventing any German counter-attack. Even though the plan of attack had to be abandoned within minutes of hitting the beaches, the 4th Division got close to all their D-Day objectives. They got their men ashore at an astonishing speed. In fifteen hours, more than 20,000 American troops landed on Utah Beach, along with 1,700 vehicles. Jodl estimated that it would take the Allies six or seven days to put three divisions into France. The Americans did that on Utah Beach in one day.

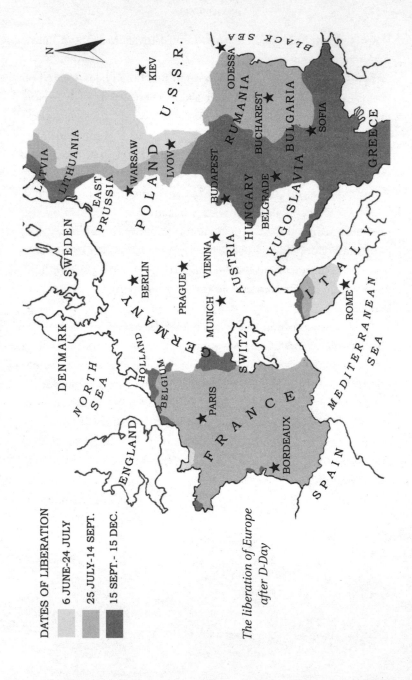

DATES OF LIBERATION

6 JUNE–24 JULY

25 JULY–14 SEPT.

15 SEPT.–15 DEC.

The liberation of Europe after D-Day

N

BLACK SEA

ODESSA

KIEV

RUMANIA

BUCHAREST

BULGARIA

SOFIA

U.S.S.R.

LATVIA

LITHUANIA

EAST PRUSSIA

WARSAW

POLAND

LVOV

BUDAPEST

HUNGARY

BELGRADE

YUGOSLAVIA

GREECE

SWEDEN

VIENNA

AUSTRIA

ITALY

ROME

BERLIN

PRAGUE

MUNICH

GERMANY

SWITZ.

MEDITERRANEAN SEA

DENMARK

HOLLAND

BELGIUM

PARIS

FRANCE

BORDEAUX

SPAIN

NORTH SEA

ENGLAND

PART THREE

TOWARDS VICTORY IN EUROPE

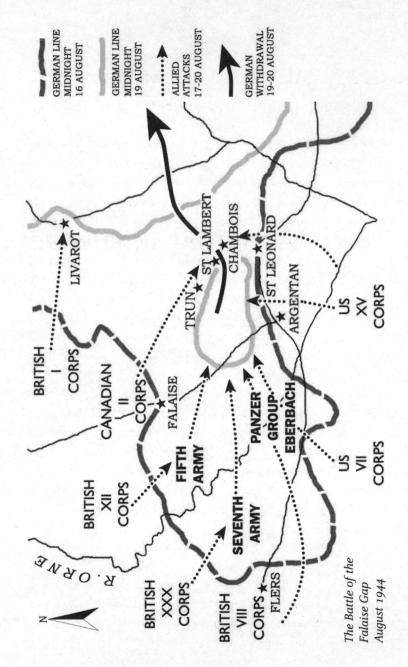

GERMAN LINE
MIDNIGHT 16 AUGUST

GERMAN LINE
MIDNIGHT 19 AUGUST

ALLIED ATTACKS
17-20 AUGUST

GERMAN WITHDRAWAL
19-20 AUGUST

N

R. ORNE

BRITISH XXX CORPS

BRITISH XII CORPS

BRITISH I CORPS

LIVAROT

CANADIAN II CORPS

FALAISE

TRUN

ST LAMBERT

CHAMBOIS

ST LEONARD

ARGENTAN

US XV CORPS

FIFTH ARMY

SEVENTH ARMY

PANZER GROUP

EBERBACH

FLERS

BRITISH VIII CORPS

US VII CORPS

*The Battle of the
Falaise Gap
August 1944*

202

11

FALAISE AND AFTER

DESPITE THE HEAVY CASUALTIES on Omaha Beach, the D-Day landings were an enormous success. The Allied planners had feared that the greatest threat to the operation was a swift German counter-attack. It never came. This was partly because of Operation Fortitude. The German High Command still expected an attack in the Pas de Calais and initially believed that the landings in Normandy were merely a diversion. With lines of communication cut by the French Resistance and heavy Allied bombing, confusion reigned on the German side. Rommel was in Germany for his wife's birthday and his planned interview with Hitler. Because of the Allies' control of the skies, he dared not fly back and had to make the long journey back to France by road. This left the defenders leaderless during the critical first few hours of the attack.

The man nominally in charge, Field Marshal von Rundstedt, knew exactly what to do. He realised that the scale of the airborne assault meant that the attack on Normandy was no mere diversionary tactic and, two hours before the Allies first set foot on a beach, he ordered a reserve Panzer division to move towards Caen. However, the Panzers were not under his control. They could not be moved without Hitler's authorisation and Hitler was asleep. He slept until noon.

The skies that morning were overcast and the Panzers could have moved without much harassment from the Allied air forces. But by 1600, when Hitler finally gave his approval for them to be moved, the clouds had broken up and Panzers had to hide in roadside woods until dark. For the defenders, a whole day had been lost. Nevertheless Hitler was jubilant.

'The news could not be better,' he said, when he heard of the Allied landings. 'As long they were in Britain we couldn't get at them. Now we have them where we can destroy them.'

The Nazi propaganda minister Joseph Goebbels also expressed his delight.

'Thank God, at last,' he said. 'This is the final round.'

For some time, the German High Command had watched in frustration as the Allies built their strength in Britain, untouched by the Luftwaffe or the Wehrmacht. Meanwhile, Allied bombing weakened Germany to the point where it was facing a serious petrol shortage and the endless waiting sapped the Germans' morale. Now the enemy was in the range of German guns.

However, the opportunity to drive the Allies back into the sea was quickly lost. By the end of 7 June, the invasion forces from all three British beaches had linked up to make one continuous front and British troops from Gold Beach had made contact with Americans from Omaha. Bayeux had been liberated, but the British had yet to achieve their D-Day objective: the capture of Caen. However, 156,000 troops were now ashore at the cost of some 10,000 casualties. Losses were much lower than expected.

Hitler ordered that the German defenders should cede no more land. In some ways, this was a sensible decision. The bocage country inland from the invasion beaches favoured the defenders. The Allies had to fight hedgerow by hedgerow. However, for the Germans fighting this way was not a winning strategy. They could inflict enormous casualties on the invaders, but they could not halt their advance. It also tied the hands of Rommel who, in the desert, had shown himself the master of fast, fluid, open warfare.

Rommel moved 2nd Panzer Division into the British sector and Von Rundstedt finally got Hitler's permission to move the 1st SS Panzer Division *Leibstandarte Adolf Hitler* from Belgium and 2nd SS Panzer Division *Das Reich* from Toulouse in the south. These formidable forces would be used to defend Caen. However, due to

Allied air superiority and harassment by the SAS, the journey from Toulouse took seventeen days instead of the five days Von Rundstedt had anticipated.

Rommel pinned his hopes on holding the town of Carentan at the base of the Cotentin Peninsula, preventing the US VII Corps from Utah Beach joining up with V Corps from Omaha. But the commander of 91st Air Landing Division holding Carentan was ambushed and killed by American troops. However, the German 6th Parachute Regiment put up stiff resistance and it was not until the morning of 10 June that the patrols from the two divisions linked up. Rommel moved the II Parachute Corps and the elite 17th SS Panzergrenadier Division into the area. But again their movement was hampered by the Allied air forces and the Resistance. The Panzergrenadiers only reached their positions southwest of Carentan on the evening of 11 June, by which time the situation was desperate. The Luftwaffe took to the air that night to drop eighteen tons of ammunition to 6th Parachute Regiment at Carentan. It was not enough to save them. Supported by a massive artillery bombardment from naval and field guns, the 101 Airborne Division attacked at dawn on 12 June and overran the town. A counter-attack by 17th SS Panzergrenadiers was repulsed as troops from Utah Beach arrived. The forces from all the Allied beaches then joined up to form one continuous front.

The US V Corps also began a sustained push southwards towards St Lô on 12 June, but found themselves facing stiff opposition in the bocage. On 15 June, the 29th Division found itself halted five miles from St Lô. Meanwhile the British had exploited the gap between the German 352nd Division, which had been driven back from Omaha Beach, and the Panzer Lehr only to stall after the battle of Villers-Bocage which cost the British twenty Cromwell tanks.

While the Allied advance to the south and east had been halted, General Joseph 'Lightin' Joe' Collins struck out westwards across the foot of the Cotentin Peninsula, reaching the west coast at Barneville on 17 June. Rommel wanted the German units in the area to save themselves by retreating to the south, or at the very least to fall back on Cherbourg. Hitler countermanded this and ordered them to stay where they were. As a result they were destroyed as the Americans fought their way up the peninsula. The success of this operation meant the entire Allied army in Normandy could turn and face southwards. By 17 June, 557,000 Allied troops had been landed, along with 81,000 vehicles and 183,000 tons of supplies. Already they outnumbered the German troops they faced, though the British in the east faced a greater concentration of armour. Fresh Allied troops coming in outnumbered the casualties being sent home. Casualty rates could still be high, though; the US 82nd Airborne had lost 1,259 on D-Day alone and sustained a casualty rate of 46 per cent before they were relieved in early July. The Allies were now in a position where exhausted units could be withdrawn and replaced. There was no shortage of ammunition and supplies and, although the Allies had failed to make a decisive breakout, the odds were very much in their favour.

Having put all their effort into fighting the invaders on the beaches, the Germans had squandered a lot of their strength. They had lost 26,000 men, including one army corps commander and five divisional commanders. Casualties outstripped their replacement rate and their armoured strength was being inexorably whittled away by air and artillery bombardment. Ninety per cent of the railways in Normandy had been knocked out by the Allied air forces and the Resistance, and the German front line troops soon grew short of fuel and ammunition.

While Hitler still held his Fifteenth Army in reserve, ready to repel any attack on the Pas de Calais, he brought in 9th and 10th SS Panzer Divisions from the Eastern Front. Two more divisions were moved up from the south of France and elements of the Fifteenth Army were moved into Normandy to be replaced by units brought in from Scandinavia. Seven armoured divisions would now be readied for the counter-attack, while the troops already engaged held the invaders where they were. While on paper, this strategy looked as if the Germans would have no trouble pushing the Allies into the sea, Von Rundstedt and Rommel were far from convinced. They knew from experience that the new units would arrive late and understrength, and Allied firepower would quickly cut them down to size. When they expressed their doubts, Hitler flew to France from his Wolf's Lair headquarters in East Prussia. The meeting took place at Soissons north-east of Paris on 17 June. Again Hitler refused to hand over control to his officers on the spot and ordered no further retreats, no matter how dire the situation. Typically, he made the entire 1,200-mile round trip without once bothering to visit the battlefield.

Even so, the plan might have worked. With their advance halted, the Allies had, momentarily, lost the initiative. The landings were running about two days behind schedule and, when the great storm blew up on 19 June, it put the Allies even further behind. Montgomery ordered the Americans to take Cherbourg urgently. Although it fell on 27 June, sporadic resistance continued until 1 July and the Germans had so thoroughly sabotaged the port facilities that it was not up to capacity until the end of September.

Even more serious was the failure of the British to take Caen with its airfield at Caripiquet. This meant that only one fighter-bomber group could be deployed in Normandy. The situation became all the more urgent after 13 June, when V-1 rockets started falling on London. They were being launched from sites in the Pas de Calais, which could be attacked more easily if the Allies had an airbase at Carpiquet.

Montgomery gave orders for the British to take Caen. Again the plan was to outflank Caen to the west and take a high point – Hill 112 – to the south. Operation *Epsom* began on the 26 June with a bombardment by over 700 guns. But bad weather robbed them of any air support from England and only limited sorties could by flown by 83rd Group of the 2nd Tactical Air Force stationed in Normandy. Progress slowed to 2,000 yards a day. 11th Armoured Division reached the slopes of Hill 112 on 29 June, but the Germans committed three Panzer divisions to the action, forcing the British to withdraw. However, the weather began to improve, leaving the Panzers vulnerable to air attack. They were unable to take advantage of the situation with a cohesive counter-attack and the British were left with much of the ground they had gained.

With the improvement in the weather, the Allied build-up picked up speed again. By the end of June, 875,000 men had landed in Normandy, along with 150,000 vehicles. The British had taken 24,698 casualties and the Americans 37,034. Between them they had had some 79,000 replacements. But while the Americans had a further nine divisions waiting in England, along with another thir-ty-nine ready for a second invasion in the South of France, the British were running out of men. Only four British and Canadian infantry divisions and two Canadian armoured divisions remained in Britain.

This gave Montgomery a grave problem. It was vital to take Caen, but this meant that the fiercest fighting fell on the weakest of the two armies under his control. Already heavy losses were causing a breakdown of the British army's renowned regimental system. He could not afford to waste men and despite the urgings of the Americans and the Air Force to launch an all-out offensive he proceeded cautiously. By early July the Allied armies had not advanced more than fifteen miles from the beaches and occupied less than a fifth of the territory envisioned in Montgomery's original plan. General George Patton, commanding officer of the American Third Army, and General Henry Crerar, commanding officer of the First Canadian Army, were ashore, but the beachhead was too small to deploy two new armies.

Around half of the US 9th Air Force had joined 83rd Group in Normandy, but the air forces had only nineteen out of the twenty-seven airfields they had been promised. With such a narrow beach-head they risked enemy shelling on take-off and landing, and mid-air collisions. Allied commanders began to fear that the whole invasion might result in a stalemate. However, the German commanders were even more depressed than those at SHAEF. General Dollmann committed suicide. Rommel and Von Rundstedt went to the Wolf's Lair in another attempt to be allowed to control the battle on the ground. Again permission was refused. When they returned, junior officers asked for permission to give up some ground to regroup. Von Rundstedt passed their request up the chain of command but, the following day, followed it up with a phone call suggesting that Hitler sue for peace. Von Rundstedt was replaced by Field Marshal Gunther von Kluge and there was a general shake-up of German command in the west.

General Bradley tried to break out, pushing south down the west coast of the Cotentin Peninsula on 7 July, then turning eastwards toward St Lô. But, again, bocage fighting kept progress down to 2,000 yards a day. By 11 July the push had run out of steam, leaving Bradley demoralised. The only person who seemed remotely optimistic about the way things were going was Montgomery. He had a new plan to take Caen which had been suggested by Air Marshal Leigh-Mallory. Earlier that year a similar stalemate at Monte Cassino in Italy had been broken by carpet bombing the defenders.

Starting at 2150 hours on 7 July, Bomber Command dropped 2,300 tons of bombs on Caen, destroying much of the city. Although they largely missed the German defensive positions, the raid raised the British troops' morale. Many of the bombs had time-delay fuses that were set to go off as the British and Canadians attacked at 0420 hours the following morning, supported by another huge bombardment. As a result, 12th SS Panzer Division was practically wiped out. Fighting was ferocious and the Germans sustained casualty rates of up to 75 per cent. By the morning of 9 July, Caen north of the River Orne was in Allied hands. The next day the British pushed towards Hill 112 to threaten the southern part of the city.

Montgomery then ordered Bradley to push on the south, so that Patton could break out into Brittany to the west and the First Army under General Courtney Hodges was to swing eastwards through Le Mans and Alençon in Operation *Cobra*. However, first they had to take St Lô. This took eight days and was enormously costly in casualties. The liberation of St Lô was followed by torrential rain which halted any further American advance and Operation *Cobra* had to be postponed. Meanwhile, the British started Operation *Goodwood*. Following another carpet bombing, they would take the rest of Caen, then engage the German armour in the open 'tank country' to the east of the city to keep them away from the American breakout.

With the battle underway, Rommel was removed from the battlefield once again, this time because he had been badly wounded when an Allied plane attacked his staff car. On 18 July, Caen was liberated by the Canadians. The British armour moved on to the east only to find the German defences there much heavier than expected. On 20 July, while Montgomery was announcing the success of Operation *Goodwood* to the world, the British armour was halted by German anti-tank guns. In the ensuing battle 413 tanks, thirty-six per cent of the British Second Army's armour, was lost. They had progressed just seven miles at a rate, Eisenhower said, of a thousand tons of bombs a mile.

According to Montgomery's initial plan, Eisenhower should take over command on the ground in Europe on 1 August. Churchill had given Eisenhower permission to sack any British officer he found unsatisfactory and many people, including Air Marshal Tedder, were calling for Montgomery's head. But Eisenhower felt sacking Britain's most famous general would damage morale and put a dent in the Anglo-American coalition. He visited Montgomery and, later, in a letter, urged him to abandon his customary caution as the enemy was now too weak to mount an effective counter-attack.

In Germany, more robust methods were being employed in an

attempt to remove the commander seen to be responsible for the latest military failure. In the Wolf's Lair, a bomb went off under the table in Hitler's headquarters. Hitler himself was shielded from the blast by a solid oak table leg and survived. None of the senior commanders in Normandy were implicated in the plot, with the single exception of Rommel. But as a great military hero he was allowed to commit suicide rather than face a trial that might have been damaging to the regime.

Despite the catastrophic consequences of Operation *Goodwood* for the British armour, Montgomery's overall strategy worked. The Germans committed the Fifteenth Army's last armoured division, 116th Panzer, to the Caen section, leaving four US armoured divisions and thirteen infantry divisions facing weakened German forces comprising two armoured divisions and seven infantry divisions – a superiority of two to one. Everything was set for Operation *Cobra* to go ahead on 24 July.

It began, like *Goodwood*, with saturation bombing along a 7,000-yard front. The 1,500 bombers of the US 8th Air force were to take out the Panzer Lehr Division which was deployed to the west of St Lô. At the last minute, the operation was postponed due to bad weather, but the message did not get through to 335 planes who, in the poor visibility, bombed their own front-line troops. *Cobra* went ahead again the next day. On the same day, General Crerar had decided to start his advance down the Caen–Falais road in Operation *Spring*. This met fierce opposition from 1st and 9th SS Panzer and had to be called off after twenty-hours. However, the Germans assumed that *Spring* was the main offensive and they thought that the minor attack in the west the day before had been halted by their own artillery. But on 25 July, *Cobra* started up again with another saturation bombing. Again the Americans managed to bomb their own front-line, killing the chief of the US ground forces, Lieutenant-General Lesley McNair, who was the highest-ranking Allied officer killed in Europe. However, the bombing also had a devastating effect on the enemy: Panzer Lehr lost two-thirds of its men and all its tanks. On the first day, the Americans advanced 4,000 yards; on the second 8,000 yards; and on the third the 2nd Armored Division, 'Hell on Wheels', broke through into open country. The next day, VII Corps captured Coutances, opening the door to the west. Two days later, on 30 July, VIII Corps, now under the command of General Patton, seized Avranches, at the base of the Cotentin Peninsula, and there was nothing in front of him.

On 1 August, the Third Army became officially operational. In twenty-four hours, Patton pushed three divisions through a five-mile gap at Avranches, out of the bocage country of Normandy and on to the open roads of Brittany. Meanwhile the Germans realised that Operation *Cobra* was the Allies' main thrust, not *Spring*. Panzers were pulled out of the Caen area and sent to close the gap, but they could only move slowly due to lack of fuel. By this time, Operation *Fortitude* was failing. The Germans were slowly coming to doubt that an attack was coming on the Pas de Calais. The real attack had already arrived in Normandy and they began moving their forces westwards.

On 3 August Hitler ordered that the armoured divisions holding the line between the River Orne and the town of Vire be replaced with infantry divisions, freeing the armour to push westwards to Avranches and cut Patton's forces in two. That same day, Patton was given new orders too. Operation *Cobra*, in the original plan, had been designed to secure the ports of Brittany. Now Bradley ordered Patton to send only a small force into Brittany. As a consequence, some of the Brittany ports were not liberated until September. Instead Patton was to circle to the south and east, outflanking the Panzers that Hitler was sending against Avranches.

Meanwhile Bradley's V Corps and the British VIII Corps began to push towards Vire. It was tough going. VIII Corps was halted two miles outside Vire. The British XXX Corps pushed on, but made such slow progress that Montgomery replaced its commander,

Major-General Bucknall, with Lieutenant-General Brian Horrocks, who had commanded XXX Corps in North Africa. Vire eventually fell to America's XIX Corp on 6 August.

By this time the German forces were disintegrating. Although unit names and numbers remained, on the ground men fought in battle groups and had been reduced to the size of a battalion. Men often did not know where they were and commanders were changed so often that no one knew who was in charge. This did not mean they were a pushover. When the Germans turned and fought they often showed a tactical superiority, and their technically superior tanks could bring an Allied advance to a sudden halt. However, as the fighting became more mobile, the German commanders became more dependent on orders conveyed by radio. This gave the Ultra codebreakers at Bletchley Park a clearer idea of what was going on. Vehicles – even tanks – had to be abandoned due to lack of fuel. Ammunition was running low, particularly for anti-tank guns. The weather was also improving, allowing Allied air forces to attack slow-moving horse-drawn German columns. By 6 August, the German Army Group B had suffered 144,261 casualties and had only 19,914 replacements.

Hitler mustered 185 tanks and threw them at Mortain, which was held by the American VII Corps, in the kind of armoured attack that Rommel had said was doomed against Allied air power. No one, with the exception of Hitler, had any faith in the plan. The commander of 116th Panzer Division had to be replaced when he refused to join the attack.

Although Ultra gave the Allies a few hours warning of the attack, the Germans managed to take Mortain and, briefly, held the high ground to the east of the town. Forty of the seventy German tanks spearheading the attack were destroyed by the evening of 7 August and the armoured column ran out of fuel after just five miles. Meanwhile Patton was making rapid progress. By 8 August, he had taken Le Mans.

On 9 August, Hitler ordered the stalled Panzers to hold their position, while the Seventh Army were ordered to push westwards on Avranches on the 11 August. By then, no one on either side thought the Germans could win the battle of Normandy.

Through Ultra, the Allies knew Hitler's plans. A stubborn man, he was not about to order a retreat. This left his entire army in Normandy liable to be encircled. While the British and Canadians pushed south-east- and eastwards, cutting off his retreat to the Seine, Patton was told to turn northward, closing the trap.

The Canadians who were to head first for Falaise made slow progress against stiff opposition and were halted after nine miles on 11 August, only halfway to their objective. However, the following day, the American XV Corps driving up from the south reached Argentan. This gave new heart to the Canadians who pushed on, reaching Falaise on 16 August. The German Seventh Army and their Panzer support were now caught in a pocket. Their only way out was through the twelve-mile gap between Falaise and Argentan. Patton begged Bradley to push on northwards to close the gap but Bradley refused, fearing that he did not have enough men in place to resist any counter-attack such a move was bound to provoke. The Germans were not unduly worried by their encirclement. They had been surrounded before on the Eastern Front. However, the Soviets had not had the overwhelming air superiority that the Allies used to pound their dwindling numbers.

Hitler assembled his Panzer Group *Eberbach*, under General Eberbach, to make a decisive counter-attack against XV Corps in Argentan. But by the time it was in place, it amounted to no more than 4,000 men and forty-five tanks. Field Marshal von Kluge, commander of Army Group B, went missing after his car was attacked by a fighter-bomber. SS General Paul Hausser, recently promoted head of the Seventh Army, temporarily replaced him.

Even Hitler began to lose confidence when the Allies launched Operation *Dragoon*. On 15 August, the Allies began their invasion of the South of France with amphibious landings on the Cote d'Azur. Hitler said it was the worst day of his life. Originally designated Operation *Anvil*, the name had been changed to *Dragoon* by Churchill, who, favouring an attack in the Balkans, felt he had been dragooned into the attack on the South of France by the Americans.

Like the D-Day landings in Normandy, the invasion of the South of France began with an airborne assault. Despite Churchill's dire forebodings, early in the morning of 15 August, a handful of planes dropped dummy parachutists west of the port of Toulon to confuse the enemy. Meanwhile to the left of the beach, near St Tropez, Allied craft towed radar-reflecting balloons to make it appear that a huge assault force was arriving to support the airborne assault on Toulon. A French commando team came ashore and cut the road to Toulon, while another team under the movie star Douglas Fairbanks Jr, now a Lieutenant-Commander in the US Navy, landed near Cannes. They came ashore in a minefield, setting off explosions that drew German gunfire. They fled back to their boats, but were mistakenly strafed by Allied planes. Swimming back to the shore, they were captured by the Germans. But within twenty-four hours they were freed by the Allied invasion.

The 'Devil's Brigade', a Special Services unit made up of Americans and Canadians under Colonel Edwin A. Walker, landed on the Iles d'Hyères to silence the guns there that overlooked one of the beaches, but found they were dummies. However, they met stiff resistance when they moved on Port Cros, the harbour on the western island. This was overcome with the help of salvoes from the 15-inch guns of HMS *Ramillies*.

At 0430, the first of 396 Dakotas that had taken off from ten airfields in Italy was over the drop zone, the fields and vineyards around the town of Le Muy, forty miles north-east of Toulon and ten miles inland from the invasion beaches. A low-lying fog convinced some of the paratroopers they were landing in the sea and they jettisoned heavy equipment and their weapons. It also caused navigational problems for the pilots and one battalion landed ten miles from the drop zone.

At 0920, the first wave of gliders arrived. Two had already been lost on the way. The right wing of one of them had snapped off. As it rolled, it broke the tow rope and disintegrated, scattering men and equipment across the sea. No-one survived. Another broke its tow rope over the sea, but ditched safely near an Allied ship. Everyone was rescued. The remaining seventy-one dropped into the landing zone at ninety m.p.h. The paratroopers had cleared some of the 'Rommel's asparagus' in the area, but there was nothing they could do about the trees which caused a great deal of damage and loss of life.

The enemy coastal defences were pounded by naval gunfire. Minesweepers went in to clear a path close to shore. Then radio-controlled boats packed with explosives were sent in to blast a way to the beaches. They were followed by landing craft firing wave after wave of rockets. The 3rd and 45th Infantry Divisions got ashore with little trouble, but the 36th ran into an unexpected minefield on the Camel beaches and withering fire in the Camel Red sector that no amount of naval gunfire could suppress. The fighting was so intense that further waves were diverted further down the beach.

A further 332 gliders arrived at dusk and by the end of the day some 9,000 British and American soldiers were in position, along with 221 jeeps and 213 artillery pieces. The airborne operation so far had cost 434 killed and 292 injured. The following day the airborne troops took Le Muy. Further inland they took Draguigan, with the help of the Resistance, and freed members of the Maquis the Germans were holding there. They also captured Lieutenant-General Ludwig Bieringer, a corps commander, and his headquarters staff. When the lost battalion rejoined its regiment, they pushed out towards Les Arcs in the west.

On the beaches, the 36th Infantry attacked the defenders of Camel Red beach from the flank and the Allies consolidated their hold. By dusk, forward elements of the amphibious force joined up with the airborne force. By midnight on 17 August, the Seventh Army under Lieutenant-General Alexander M. 'Sandy' Patch, a veteran of Guadalcanal, had landed more than 86,500 French and American troops, 12,500 vehicles and 46,100 tons of supplies.

The Allies were also masters of the air in the South of France. Between 16 and 18 August, the Luftwaffe flew only 141 sorties. A landing craft was sunk and at dusk on 18 August five Junkers Ju 88s bombed the American command ship USS *Catoctin*. The attack killed six and wounded forty-two, but did only minor damage to the ship. After that the Luftwaffe withdrew from southern France, leaving the skies to the USAAF, who bombed bridges and strafed road and rail traffic to devastating effect.

The invaders were helped by the Resistance who were strong in the south. They had harassed Panzers moving north for the defence of Normandy, but a premature call for an armed uprising issued by mistake by de Gaulle's headquarters in London led to lightly-armed guerrillas facing armour and aircraft. The Germans also took their revenge on the civilian population, burning villages and massacring the inhabitants.

The invasion force also received invaluable information through Ultra. Bletchley Park decoded a message from General Johannes von Blaskowitz, whose Army Group G held the area from the Italian border to the Pyrenees, ordering the withdrawal of mobile forces and leaving the ports of Toulon and Marseilles defended by garrison troops. Patch gave chase with his main force, while the airborne infantry liberated Cannes and Nice and the French II Corps headed for Toulon and Marseilles.

On 16 August, Von Kluge reappeared at his headquarters in Normandy. He reported that the Falaise pocket could not be held and they had to withdraw. Finally, Hitler agreed, but it was too late. The following day a renewed push by the Canadians and the US V Corps, which had taken over from XV in the south, closed the

Falaise gap to just a few hundred yards and, despite fierce fighting, on 20 August, it was closed altogether. Von Kluge was sacked and summoned to the Wolf's Lair under suspicion of treason. Having a good idea of what was in store there for him, he committed suicide. Field Marshal Walther Model replaced him, but there was little he could do. General Eberbach managed to get some of his formations out of the Falaise pocket, but he was captured on 30 August. SS General Hausser was badly wounded and lost an eye. He escaped from the pocket, but found himself without a command. The Seventh Army was no more. Those left in the pocket were pulverised by Allied bombing. The stench of rotting flesh was so bad it could be smelt in the planes overhead. Resistance ceased on 22 August. Visiting the battlefield two days later, Eisenhower said that you could walk on the dead for hundreds of yards on end.

The destruction was so complete that it was difficult to calculate the scale of the victory. There were probably 10,000 dead. Some 20,000 had escaped, but 50,000 had surrendered, including many who were not German. The 1st Polish Armoured Division who were fighting with the Canadians under General Crerar carried truck-loads of British uniforms with them so that, when they came across *Ost* battalions, fellow Poles could quickly change sides. The Allies found 7,700 wrecked or abandoned vehicles in the pocket, not including 567 tanks or self-propelled guns, along with 950 abandoned field guns. The remnants of the eight battle groups of Panzers who had escaped could only muster seventy tanks and thirty-six field guns between them.

While the Allied air forces had been finishing off the Germans in the Falaise pocket, Patton's Third Army had been racing eastward. He crossed the Seine on 19 August. The British and Canadians turned eastwards, reaching the Seine on 25 August. Eisenhower decided that the advancing Allies should bypass Paris to avoid the destruction and loss of life a battle for the city would entail. Hitler for his part intended to turn the the city into a fortress but, given the hopelessness of the German position in France, decided to have the city burnt down.

It was the people of Paris themselves who decided the outcome. For more than four years, they had suffered the humiliation of occupation. As if to rub salt in the wounds, every day for the 1,500 days of the occupation, German troops had paraded around the Arc de Triomphe and marched down the Champs Elysées to the Place de la Concorde. Now, with the Allies on French soil, Parisians grew restive. On 10 August, French railwaymen staged the first real strike of the occupation, calling for better food in Paris and higher wages. In response, the Germans shipped their political prisoners out of the city and sent them to concentration camps where most of them died. However, 1,500 Jews found they had been granted a short reprieve when the buses assigned to transport them were sabotaged.

Electric and gas supplies in the city became sporadic and the Metro stopped running. Sensing that trouble was brewing, on 13 August the Germans started disarming the city's 20,000 gendarmes. The policemen responded by going on strike. The Resistance called on them to put aside their uniforms and keep their guns. Otherwise they would be considered traitors. 'The hour of liberation has come', they were told.

Sporadic gunfire began to be heard on the streets of Paris. The Germans reacted swiftly. The SS machine-gunned thirty-five French youths at the Carrefour de Cascades on the night of 16 August. With Paris near to insurrection, Hitler issued an order: 'Paris must not fall into enemy hands, but, if it does, he must find nothing but ruins.' The city's new commandant Lieutenant-General Dietrich von Choltitz was instructed to wreck Paris's industrial capacity, blow the bridges over the Seine and destroy the city's famous monuments. All its significant buildings were mined ready for demolition, but Von Choltitz stayed his hand. However, when German soldiers were shot at, he threatened to raze entire city blocks and kill the inhabitants in reprisal.

Swedish Consul Raoul Nordling intervened to calm the situation and Field Marshal Model gave Von Choltitz permission to delay destroying the bridges, which might still be needed in his withdrawal from France. And there seemed no point in inflaming the citizenry, if the city was still to be defended. Von Choltitz still had fifty tanks and garrison of 22,000 troops. He had been promised another division, which would have made the city a costly objective to take.

The Communists planned an uprising. To pre-empt this the Gaullist Resistance organised 2,000 striking policemen to seize the Préfecture de Police near Notre Dame. They hoisted the Tricolor and sang the 'Marseillaise'. Next, they took the Palais de Justice and, when German tanks appeared in the Boulevard de Palais, they were fired upon.

The following day, 20 August, the Gaullists seized the Hôtel de Ville. Nordling had an urgent meeting with Von Choltitz where the commandant granted the Resistance fighters combat status. They would be allowed to hold the buildings they occupied, provided they did not attack the German stronghold in the centre of the city. But the truce could not hold. On the left bank and in other areas no longer under German control the revolutionary cry 'Aux barricades!' went up. The cobblestones were torn up and hundreds of barricades, made from overturned vehicles and felled trees, were manned by Parisians in makeshift uniforms.

The Germans fought back, half-heartedly. While tanks machine-gunned buildings, no high-explosive rounds were fired. Their tactics were largely defensive and they never pressed home their attacks. Only the SS seemed to be spoiling for a fight. While the French took prisoners, they murdered theirs.

By 22 August, there was open warfare on the streets of Paris in at least three areas. The Resistance begged the Americans for help. Eisenhower ordered Bradley to take the city, fearing that the Germans would use aircraft and tanks against the populace with huge loss of life. By the night of 23 August, the Grand Palais was on fire, hit by an incendiary round and five hundred Parisians were dead. The Resistance seized the mairies, the borough town halls. The Germans responded by using tanks to machine-gun them. Nevertheless, aside from the Germans' central stronghold, the city appeared to be almost entirely in the hands of the Resistance.

For political reasons, Eisenhower had already ordered that the first unit into Paris was to be the 2nd Free French Armoured Division under Major-General Philippe Leclerc. He sent a message dropped by plane to the Préfecture saying, 'Hold on we are coming'.

However, he made slow progress, losing 300 men, forty tanks and over a hundred other vehicles in the first day. V Corps commander Major-General Leonard Gerow asked Bradley for permission to send his 4th Infantry Division, which had landed at Utah Beach, to join the assault on Paris. Bradley said, 'To hell with prestige, tell the 4th to slam on in and take the liberation.'

On the night of 24 August, Leclerc infiltrated an advanced party into the city. At 2122, six half-tracks and three tanks arrived at the Hôtel de Ville. Their presence was announced by the ringing of church bells. Von Choltitz called Field Marshal Model's headquarters and held the phone to the window so that they could hear the bells announcing the liberation.

The following morning – D+80 – Leclerc's main force swept into the city from the south-west, while the US 4th Infantry liberated the east. By 1000 only a few pockets of German resistance remained. Von Choltitz did nothing to further the fighting. On hearing that the Allies had entered the city, Hitler asked, 'Is Paris burning?' Von Choltitz gave no orders to fire the demolition charges and signed documents surrendering the city to Leclerc, then jointly to Leclerc and the Resistance, who had sustained over 2,500 casualties with around 1,000 dead. Some 10,000 Germans were taken prisoner, along with thirty-six tanks.

By noon, Tricolors fluttered from the Arc de Triomphe and the

Eiffel Tower. The next day, the Free French leader General Charles de Gaulle, who had set up a new administration in Bayeux in June, made a triumphal entry to the city to take control. But Hitler still wanted Paris to burn. That night, the Luftwaffe dropped incendiaries, burning down 500 houses, killing fifty and injuring 500. For Paris it was the worst air raid of the war. Later, on 6 September, the first V-2 rocket would be fired against Paris.

On 27 August, Bradley and Eisenhower entered the city and on 29 August, the US 28th Division made a triumphal march through the city. Meanwhile to the south there had been heavy fighting. Although Toulon and Marseilles were lightly defended by Normandy standards, the Free French faced stiff resistance there. Only the use of heavy naval bombardment allowed them to overcome the Germans and on 28 August, both ports fell into Allied hands. By then, the Allies had caught up with Montgomery's original invasion schedule.

During the battle of Normandy, thirty-eight Allied divisions had seen off fifty-one German divisions, though SHAEF computed the Germans' actual combat strength to be equivalent to thirty-three divisions. The cost to the Allies was 209,672 casualties, including 36,976 dead. Another 16,714 aircrew had been lost in the 4,101 aircraft downed over the battlefield. German dead and wounded amounted to some 240,000, along with 200,000 missing or captured. They lost over 3,600 aircraft, 1,500 tanks, 3,500 guns and 20,000 vehicles. Meanwhile, as the Germans fell back in disarray, the Allies grew stronger. By the end of August, they had landed 2,052,299 men, 438,471 vehicles and 3,098,259 tons of stores. Another 380,000 men, 69,000 vehicles, 306,000 tons of supplies and 18,000 tons of fuel had been landed on the Dragoon beaches.

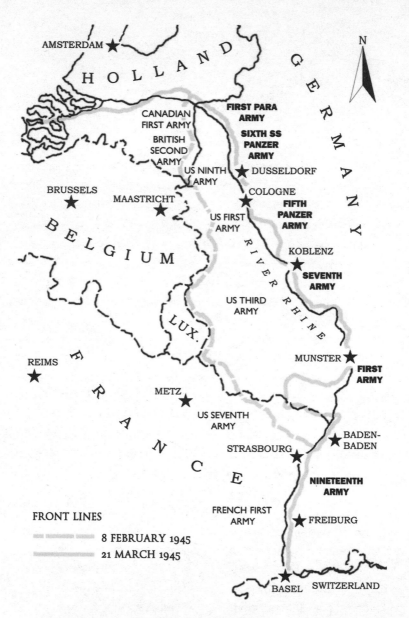

The Allies cross the Rhine
February–March 1945

12

THE SUCCESS OF THE SECOND FRONT

ONCE THE BATTLE of Normandy was won and Paris liberated, nobody doubted that Germany had lost the war, though there were several competing ideas about how the final victory would be won. The US Seventh Army chased von Blaskowitz up the entire length of France. The German retreat was hampered by the Resistance, but von Blaskowitz, in turn, slowed General Patch's advance by delaying actions.

He turned to fight at the ancient city of Besançon to gain time for a final withdrawal through the Belfort gap into Alsace and back into Germany. Three thousand German troops massed to face the Americans there. On 7 September, after two days of fierce fighting, the Americans took the city, but still ferocious German resistance halted their advance. After taking Toulon and Marseilles, the French II Corps had sped up the Rhône valley to Lyon. They liberated Dijon on 10 September, taking tens of thousands of prisoners, largely East Europeans including a battalion of Ukrainians who killed their German officers and switched sides. The German troops, however, pulled back in good order. Then on 12 September, Leclerc's Armoured Division which had fought its way across from Normandy arrived in Dijon, establishing one single front extending from the English Channel to the Swiss border.

On 1 September 1944, Eisenhower had taken over formal command of all ground forces in Western Europe from General Montgomery, who had wanted to see the invasion through to the bitter end. He planned to keep the two Army Groups together, with the 21st – the British and the Canadians – sweeping up the Channel coast to seize Antwerp, while Bradley's 12th Army Group moved through Belgium to enter Germany north of the Ardennes. This would clear the Channel coast of V-2 rocket sites.

By this time, V-2s were raining down on London. They carried 900kg of high explosives and there was no defence against them. Hitler's latest vengeance weapon was causing huge civilian casualties, which was bad enough. But if they were turned against the Channel ports, they would disrupt the army's supply lines. Another of Montgomery's aims was to seize Antwerp. Currently supplies had to be transported by truck from the Normandy coast. Taking the Belgium port would solve the Allies' growing logistical problems. Montgomery's plan would also put the Allied armies in the Ruhr, Germany's industrial heartland, the final objective of Operation Overlord.

However, Montgomery was not popular with the American generals who found him too cautious. Already Bradley's Army Group was bigger than Montgomery's. Four American divisions were now arriving in Europe each month and the Americans would eventually outnumber the British and Canadians four to one. American public opinion also felt that there should be a change.

When Eisenhower took over, Churchill promoted Montgomery to the rank of Field Marshal in compensation. This was one rank higher than Eisenhower. The American army had no equivalent and the new five-star rank of General of the Army had to be quickly invented. Meanwhile, Patton's Third Army crossed the River Meuse at Verdun on 31 August and was already beginning to cross the Moselle River near Metz on 5 September, with the possibility of achieving a breakthrough into Germany's economically important Saarland.

But Eisenhower had a problem. The ports in Brittany were not yet secure and supplies were running short. So he abandoned the original Overlord plan of advancing on a broad front (it had originally been feared that a narrow front would be too vulnerable to counter-attack) and allowed Montgomery his thrust to the north-east. The British Second Army liberated Brussels on 3 September and Antwerp the next day. However, this starved Patton of the supplies he needed to advance into Germany.

With Antwerp in Allied hands, the original plan was to be resumed and Eisenhower could not longer justify diverting supplies to Montgomery at Patton's expense. In a final attempt to have his own way, Montgomery attempted to seize a bridgehead over the Rhine at Arnhem. On 17 September, in Operation *Market Garden*, three divisions of the British 1st Airborne were dropped in a 'carpet' across northern Holland to clear the way for the Second Army. But the Germans were just able to check the thrust, cutting off the paratroopers and taking many of them prisoner. This was the normally cautious Montgomery's first and only defeat in a major battle, though, characteristically, he described it as a 'ninety per cent success'.

By the end of September, the Allied advance was slowing due to a storage of fuel. This gave the Germans time to regroup and the German defence rapidly stiffened as the Allies approached the frontiers of Germany itself. The US First Army spent a month grinding down the defences of Aachen. It fell on 20 October, the first German city to fall to the Allies. However, the First Canadian Army, on the left of the British Second, did not clear the Schelde estuary west of Antwerp, until early November. And Patton's Third Army remained held up before Metz.

The Allies had made an amazing advance of 350 miles in just a few weeks after the break-out from Normandy, but now they were at a halt. They had a superiority over the Germans of twenty to one in tanks and twenty-five to one in aircraft. But none of SHAEF's planners had anticipated such a rapid German collapse. They did not have the logistical support to make a rapid thrust into Germany itself. If the Allies had been prepared, they could have taken the Ruhr and Saarland, but in November 1944 both the Ruhr Valley and the Saarland remained in Germany hands.

Hitler seized the moment. Despite the inexorable advance by the Red Army to the east, he still believed that the war would be won or lost in the west. In October, he had raised a *Volkssturm*, or 'home guard,' for the defence of the Third Reich, conscripting all able-bodied men between the ages of sixteen and sixty. The fruit of this second 'total mobilisation' he concentrated on the western borders of Germany itself.

By mid-November there were six Allied armies massed on the Western Front. Forty-eight divisions were spread along a 600-mile front extending from the North Sea to Switzerland. They launched a general offensive. The American Seventh Army and the French First Army pushed forward to the Rhine River in Alsace, but elsewhere there were only small gains. Although Germany was now starved of material resources, with its newly-raised manpower, reserves and the troops that had made their way back from France, the German build-up was by now progressing faster than that of the Allies. In mid-December 1944, this gave the Germans one last chance to launch a sizeable counter-offensive. Von Rundstedt was reinstated as commander of the army in the west, but played little part in the 'Rundstedt Offensive', also known as the Ardennes Offensive and to the Germans as Operation *Herbstnebel* (Autumn Fog), but better known by Churchill's dismissive title 'The Battle of the Bulge'. Churchill had, in fact, first used the term in May 1940 when Von Rundstedt had launched his successful assault in the same area. Hitler amassed twenty-four divisions. On 16 December they attacked through the wooded hill country of the Ardennes against the US First Army who were weakest in that sector of the front. The Allies' advantage of overwhelming air superiority was lost due to bad weather. The Fifth Panzer Army, under the talented commander General Hasso von Manteuffel, was to cross the Meuse and drive on Brussels, while the Sixth SS Panzer Army to its right, under SS General Sepp Dietrich, was to retake Antwerp. The aim was to cut off the British and Canadian forces at the northern end of the front from their supplies and crush them, while the American forces to the south would be held at bay by the German left.

For once the offensive came as a complete surprise to the Allies. Mist and rain limited the effectiveness of air reconnaissance. Eight German armoured divisions attacked along a seventy-five-mile front. The Fifth Panzer Army penetrated to within twenty miles of the crossings of the Meuse. However, the American 101st Airborne stood firm at Bastogne. By Christmas the German drive had penetrated about sixty-five miles into the Allied lines but the front had narrowed to just twenty miles across. Montgomery took charge of the situation in the north and swung his reserves southward to stop the Germans reaching the Meuse. Bradley, in the south, sent the Third Army under Patton to relieve Bastogne, which he achieved on 26 December. Then the weather cleared. Five thousand Allied planes bombed and strafed the German attackers and their supply train. By 8 January, the German thrust risked being cut off in its turn and they were forced to withdraw. Although the offensive come as a shock to the Allies and inflicted a great deal of damage – the Americans alone sustained 75,000 casualties – it had exhausted the Germans who lost 120,000 and had little strength left to offer any resistance later. By 16 January, the Germans were on the back foot again.

With the German counter-offensive crushed, Montgomery began to build up the strength of his forces in the northern sector of the front ready to cross the Rhine. Although less generously supplied, American generals also moved forward. Patton's Third Army hit the Rhine at Koblenz early in March. General Courtney H. Hodges' First Army took the bridge over the Rhine at Remagen and crossed the river, and Lieutenant-General William H. Simpson's Ninth Army hit the Rhine near Düsseldorf. But the three American armies were ordered to hold their position until Montgomery was ready and spent their time clearing the west bank of the river.

On the night of 22 March, Patton could hold off no longer. The

Third Army crossed the Rhine at Oppenheim, between Mannheim and Mainz, practically unopposed. The following night, after wave after wave of bombers went in and the east bank of the river was blasted by more than 3,000 guns, Montgomery sent twenty-five divisions over a thirty-mile stretch of the Rhine near Wesel. German resistance was slight but, after Arnhem, Montgomery had regained his customary caution and consolidated a bridgehead twenty miles deep before sending in more troops. While the Canadian First Army pushed north through the Netherlands, the British Second Army drove across northern Germany to Lübeck and to Wismar on the Baltic. At the same time the American armies swept across southern Germany, taking Magdeburg and Leipzig and pushing on to the borders of Czechoslovakia and Austria.

The German Chief of Staff, General Heinz Guderian, wanted to move Germany's forces eastward to hold off the Red Army that was now advancing on Berlin, but Hitler wanted to commit his last reserve – the Eleventh and Twelfth Armies – to pushing the Western Allies back over the Rhine and Guderian was sacked. Neither the German people nor the army shared Hitler's enthusiasm. With the war lost, they want to see the Western Allies move eastward quickly to take Berlin and occupy as much of the country as possible before the Soviets did. Nor did they share Hitler's desire for more destruction. On the eve of the Rhine crossing, 19 March, Hitler had ordered that the fighting should continue 'without consideration for our own population'. His idea was to create a desert in front of the western invaders and his regional commissioners were instructed to destroy industrial plants, electricity works, gas works, waterworks and any remaining stores of food and clothing.

'If the war is lost, the German nation will also perish,' Hitler said, 'so there is no need to consider what the people require for continued existence.'

Hitler's minister of production, Albert Speer, was appalled at such callousness and persuaded the army and industrial leaders not to implement Hitler's decree. Driving eastward from the Rhine, the Western Allies met little opposition and reached the Elbe River sixty miles from Berlin on 11 April, where they halted.

The Red Army had crossed the Oder River, which marks the post-war boundary between Poland and Germany, in early March. To the south, they reached Vienna on 6 April and Königsberg on 9 April. On 16 April, the Red Army crossed the River Neisse and within a week they had reached the outskirts of Berlin.

Hitler remained in Berlin, hoping for a miracle. The death of President Roosevelt on 12 April brought a temporary glimmer of hope, but did not materially alter the situation. By 25 April, the Red Army encircled Berlin and linked up with the Americans on the Elbe River. On April 30 Hitler committed suicide in the ruins of his Chancellery with advancing Soviet troops less than half a mile from his bunker. Hitler's successor, Admiral Karl Dönitz, used the next few weeks to move as many German civilians and troops to the west. Before the final surrender, he managed to get fifty-five per cent of the eastern army – 1,800,000 men – out of the Soviet zone and into the area controlled by the British, Americans and French.

The formal surrender of the German forces in Northern Europe was signed in Montgomery's headquarters on Lüneburg Heath on 4 May. Another document, covering all the German forces, was signed at Eisenhower's headquarters at Reims in the presence of a Soviet delegation and, at midnight on 8 May 1945, the war in Europe was officially at an end.

Although the Western Allies had not reached Berlin before the Soviets, the second front must be judged a success. While the Western Allies lost large numbers of men initially, the suffered nothing like the losses experienced by the Red Army as they pushed westwards. And although there has been a great deal of criticism of Montgomery's handling of the D-Day landings, as he would have carried the blame if the Allies had lost the Battle of Normandy, he should take the credit for winning it.

Viewed from the German side, the responsibility for losing the Battle of Normandy, and subsequently the war, sits squarely on Hitler's shoulders. He relied on fortifications and mines rather than well-trained, well-motivated soldiers. Instead of giving his commanders on the ground a free hand, or even room to manoeuvre, he directed the battle from his headquarters in East Prussia, over 600 miles away in what is now Poland, poring over maps. Even when he did go to France, he was never went closer to the front than 150 miles.

On 6 June itself, a rapid response to the D-Day landings was delayed because Hitler was asleep. Even when he did awake, he delayed giving permission for the Panzers to move until 1600, by which time the skies over Normandy were clear and they could not move without danger of being attacked.

Later that afternoon, Hitler ordered the use of V-1 weapons against London. This was not an appropriate response. First, it would take six days to move the launchers from the heavily camouflaged depots to the Channel coast. Next, although the V-1 flew fast enough to make it difficult for Allies anti-aircraft gunners or fighter planes to shoot them down, they were unreliable and often wildly inaccurate. On the first day of the V-1 offensive, ten were launched. Four crashed immediately, two disappeared completely, three landed in open fields and one demolished a railway bridge. Of the 8,000 launched over the ensuing months, only twenty-four per cent hit their target. With the Allies pouring troops across the Channel, it would have made more strategic sense to use these new weapons against the bridgeheads, the Mulberry Harbours and the Channel ports. Only later were they used against Antwerp.

While Hitler interfered with his commanders at every level, Roosevelt and Churchill, although they had grave doubts about the Normandy landings, made no attempt to tell their admirals and generals what to do. Even Eisenhower, who was Supreme Commander of the Allied Expedition Force, left decisions to his subordinates. When his naval aide, Harry Butcher, went to Eisenhower's trailer on the morning of 6 June to tell him that the landings had started, he found Eisenhower reading a cowboy novel and smoking a cigarette. When he got up, Eisenhower walked over to the tent that was headquarters of SHAEF's operations centre and sat in on a discussion about when they should release the news of the invasion. Montgomery had been adamant that they should wait until the beachhead was secure, Eisenhower offered no opinion. Later he wrote a note to his superior, General George Marshall, chairman of the Joint Chiefs of Staff, to tell him that everything was going well.

Later he visited Montgomery, but there was no time to chat as the British general was packing ready to move his headquarters across the Channel. Eisenhower then went to see Admiral Ramsay who reported that everything was going well with the naval operation. At midday, he looked in on the operations tent again and heard the disturbing news of the problems on Omaha Beach. Afterwards he briefed a few journalists – at one point looking out of the door and remarking, 'The sun is shining.'

He spent the rest of the day anxiously listening to reports coming in from the beaches, his mood swinging from jubilation to depression. After dinner, he went to bed early. So on D-Day, Eisenhower, the Allied Supreme Commander, gave no orders, while Hitler gave two bad ones.

The Western Allies had learnt the lessons that Hitler had taught them with his *Blitzkrieg* earlier in the war. They had seen that combined operations, co-ordinating the infantry, armoured columns, air attacks and airborne assaults won the day. In North Africa, then in Sicily and Italy, the Allies had added the use of sea power to the mix and the landing craft the Americans had designed for use in the Pacific. Meanwhile, Hitler had forgotten everything he had learnt earlier in the war.

After delaying Von Rundstedt's advance, Hitler then repeatedly ordered that there should be no retreat, despite the advice of his generals. He sought to fight a static war rather than the open, mobile war that had been perfected in the tactics of *Blitzkrieg*. After the Normandy landings, the German forces had plenty of time to pull back to the Seine and form a strong defensive barrier line there, but Hitler would have none of it. Because of Hitler's belief that the main Allied attack would come in the Pas de Calais, he fed the German armoured forces into the Battle of Normandy piecemeal. Once they were there, they were kept there by his 'no retreat' order until they collapsed or were trapped. His infantry divisions suffered the same fate. Those who escaped had to retreat mainly on foot and were soon overtaken by American and British mechanised columns. Despite their counter-attacks, the Germans had no real faith that they could turn the tide once the Battle of Normandy was lost. The Battle of the Bulge was only a limited success because bad weather denied the Allies the use of their air forces. Once they could fly again, German resistance collapsed. By the time the Allies approached the German border at the beginning of September, there was no organised resistance left to prevent them driving directly on into the heart of Germany.

Air power was a key factor in the Allies' favour, but the Germans could have challenged the Allied air forces over the skies of Europe if they had employed more Messerschmitt Me 262s, the first military jet attack aircraft, in a fighter role, something Hitler himself delayed, insisting that the Me 262 be developed as a bomber. The German Tiger tank was also superior to anything the Allies possessed, but they would have been better deployed if they had been mixed in with weaker infantry formations. Instead they were kept in 'showcase' units which could be easily countered by air attacks and artillery. Artillery, particularly naval artillery, was also decisive on D-Day itself. The Germans could not match the Allied naval power. After 1942, the German surface fleet rarely put to sea. In May 1943, German U-boats had suffered such a heavy defeat that they had to be withdrawn from the Battle of the Atlantic. There were too few left to menace the invasion fleet.

Throughout the war, Allied – especially British – intelligence was far superior to that possessed by the Germans. Much of the success of D-Day can be attributed to Operation Fortitude which led Hitler to believe, even weeks after the invasion, that the assault on Normandy was merely a diversion and the real attack would come on the Pas de Calais. The breaking of the German Enigma code by the code-breakers at Bletchley Park was also vital. It allowed those running Fortitude to judge how effective they were being and it allowed the Allies to know in advance the Germans' plans for their counter-attacks once they were ashore.

But most of all, the credit must go to the fighting spirit of the young men who went ashore on 6 June 1944. Most of them were green troops who had not seen action before, but they had been trained well and each part of the operation had been meticulously planned. Even so, things went wrong, as they are bound to in battle, but the Allied troops had no fear of showing initiative. Senior officers such as General Roosevelt showed no compunction in abandoning a carefully-laid plan when it was shown to have gone awry: Patton and even Montgomery, later, would deliberately disobey orders if they considered that it was the right thing to do. The young men under their command had great faith in their commanders. They also believed in what they were doing. Hitler, in their eyes, was an unspeakable evil and many would pay with their lives to put an end to him and his murderous regime. In the story of D-Day and the fighting that followed, there are an enormous number of examples of heroism – men who knowingly sacrificed their lives for their comrades. Such men cannot be beaten.

On the other side, a great many of the defenders of the Atlantic Wall were eastern Europeans who knew little of the German war aims and cared even less. Alongside them were battle-hardened German troops who had seen action on the Eastern Front, but many of them were disillusioned. After overrunning the west of Europe in a matter of weeks in 1940, the Wehrmacht expected an easy victory in the east. What they got was years of fighting in appalling conditions against a fanatical enemy for a leader who did not seem to care how many died. Many Germans were happy to surrender. Only the most dedicated Nazis were prepared to die.

Even with the benefit of hindsight, it is difficult to assess how history would have been changed if the Allies had not invaded Normandy. If all the men and materiel expended in Normandy had been deployed on the Italian front, progress there would have been made much more rapidly. However, even once the whole of Italy had fallen, the Allies would have had the superhuman task of getting their armies over the Alps. Without a second front in France or the Low Countries, it seems certain that, once the Red Army had taken Berlin, it would have continued its advance to the Atlantic coast. If the British and Americans had not invaded, Stalin, who had been urging the opening of a second front since 1942, would have seen no reason to allow an Allied presence on the Continent, north of the Alps, after the end of the war.

However, without an invasion from the west, Hitler could have turned his V-1s and V-2s on Russia, forcing the Soviets to halt. Stalin and Hitler had had a pact earlier in the war and it would perhaps not have been impossible for them to contrive another. Without an invasion of France, a considerable rift would have developed between the British and the Americans. This would certainly have weakened the war effort in the Far East, so the outcome of the war both in Europe and the Pacific could have hung in the balance.

It is even conceivable that, if the invasion had not stopped Hitler using his V-1s and V-2s against London, the British might have been forced to capitulate, and plans had already been made for a successor to the V-2 which would have been able to reach New York. In the worst case scenario, without a second front, or its failure, the Allies might have lost the Second World War.

BIBLIOGRAPHY

Ambrose, Stephen E., *D-Day – The Climatic Battle of World War II*, Simon & Schuster, New York, 1994.

Badsey, Stephen, *Normandy 1944 – Allied Landings and Breakout*, Osprey, London, 1990.

Brown, David, ed., *Invasion Europe*, HMSO, London, 1994.

Bruce, George, *Second Front Now!*, MacDonald & Jane's, London, 1979.

Collier, Richard, *D-Day – June 6, 1944*, Cassell, London, 1992.

Goldsmith, Maurice, *Sage: A Life of J.D. Bernal*, Hutchinson, London, 1980.

Hastings, Max, *Overlord*, Michael Joseph, London, 1984.

Haswell, Rock, *The Intelligence and Deception of the D-Day Landings*, BT Batsford Ltd, London, 1979.

Hawkins, Desmond, *War Report D-Day to VE Day*, Ariel Books, London, 1985.

Keegan, John, *Six Armies in Normandy*, Jonathan Cape, London, 1982.

Kemp, Anthony, *D-Day – The Normandy Landings and the Liberation of Europe*, Thames & Hudson, London, 1994.

Kershaw, Robert J., *D-Day – Piercing the Atlantic Wall*, Ian Allan Publishing, Shepperton, 1993.

Kirkpatrick, Charles et al. *D-Day*, Salamander Books Ltd, London, 1999.

Kilvert-Jones, Tim, *Sword Beach*, Leo Cooper, London, 2001.

Miller, Russell, *Nothing Less Than Victory: The Oral History of D-Day*, Penguin, London, 1993.

Paine, Lauran, *D-Day*, Robert Hale Ltd, London, 1981.

Ryan, Cornelius, *The Longest Day*, Coronet, London, 1993.

Turner, John Frayn, *Invasion '44 – The Full Story of D-Day*, Airlife, Shrewsbury, 1994.

Warner, Philip, *The D-Day Landings*, William Kimber, London, 1980.

Wilson, Theodore A., ed., *D-Day 1944*, University Press of Kansas, Lawrence, Kansas, 1994.

INDEX OF ARMIES, BATTLES, CAMPAIGNS & COMMANDERS